Samuel French Acting Edition

Pilots of the Purple Twilight

by Steve Kluger

SAMUELFRENCH.COM   SAMUELFRENCH.CO.UK

Copyright © 1987, 1988, 1999 by Steve Kluger
All Rights Reserved

PILOTS OF THE PURPLE TWILIGHT is fully protected under the copyright laws of the United States of America, the British Commonwealth, including Canada, and all other countries of the Copyright Union. All rights, including professional and amateur stage productions, recitation, lecturing, public reading, motion picture, radio broadcasting, television and the rights of translation into foreign languages are strictly reserved.

ISBN 978-0-573-62681-4

www.SamuelFrench.com
www.SamuelFrench.co.uk

For Production Enquiries

United States and Canada
Info@SamuelFrench.com
1-866-598-8449

United Kingdom and Europe
Plays@SamuelFrench.co.uk
020-7255-4302

Each title is subject to availability from Samuel French, depending upon country of performance. Please be aware that *PILOTS OF THE PURPLE TWILIGHT* may not be licensed by Samuel French in your territory. Professional and amateur producers should contact the nearest Samuel French office or licensing partner to verify availability.

CAUTION: Professional and amateur producers are hereby warned that *PILOTS OF THE PURPLE TWILIGHT* is subject to a licensing fee. Publication of this play(s) does not imply availability for performance. Both amateurs and professionals considering a production are strongly advised to apply to Samuel French before starting rehearsals, advertising, or booking a theatre. A licensing fee must be paid whether the title(s) is presented for charity or gain and whether or not admission is charged. Professional/Stock licensing fees are quoted upon application to Samuel French.

No one shall make any changes in this title(s) for the purpose of production. No part of this book may be reproduced, stored in a retrieval system, or transmitted in any form, by any means, now known or yet to be invented, including mechanical, electronic, photocopying, recording, videotaping, or otherwise, without the prior written permission of the publisher. No one shall upload this title(s), or part of this title(s), to any social media websites.

For all enquiries regarding motion picture, television, and other media rights, please contact Samuel French.

MUSIC USE NOTE

Licensees are solely responsible for obtaining formal written permission from copyright owners to use copyrighted music in the performance of this play and are strongly cautioned to do so. If no such permission is obtained by the licensee, then the licensee must use only original music that the licensee owns and controls. Licensees are solely responsible and liable for all music clearances and shall indemnify the copyright owners of the play(s) and their licensing agent, Samuel French, against any costs, expenses, losses and liabilities arising from the use of music by licensees. Please contact the appropriate music licensing authority in your territory for the rights to any incidental music.

IMPORTANT BILLING AND CREDIT REQUIREMENTS

If you have obtained performance rights to this title, please refer to your licensing agreement for important billing and credit requirements.

NOTE: The George M. Cohan songs performed in *Pilots of the Purple Twilight* are in the public domain and are thus free from any copyright restrictions. For access to some of the lesser-known titles, producers are referred to the Columbia original cast recording of *George M!*, which contains all of the songs used herein.

PILOTS OF THE PURPLE TWILIGHT was first presented on October 2, 1989, at the Theatre of Newburyport in Newburyport, Massachusetts, under the direction of Kerry Fusaro.

Cast

John Jacob Astor	ROBERT HEINLEIN
Isidor Straus	JOHN DAVIN
J. Bruce Ismay	JEREM GOODWIN
First Officer William Murdoch	STAN BOCKO
Alice Fortune	JOSIE McELROY
Charley Fortune	JOHN KOOI
Thomas Kilgannon	KERRY FUSARO
Ida Straus	MARA CLARKE
Mary Canavan	JOAN KIRSCHNER

CHARACTERS

JOHN JACOB ASTOR: late 40's and a born aristocrat, he subscribes to the belief that "a man who owns a million dollars is as well off as if he were rich."

ISIDOR STRAUS: mid-60's and a self-made man, having climbed the social ladder by dint of hard work and long hours, he does not have much patience with Astor or any others who inherited their fortunes and their positions in the upper class.

J. BRUCE ISMAY: 40-50 and the prissy Chairman of the Board of the White Star Line, he'd prefer not to acknowledge anyone below the rank of a belted earl.

FIRST OFFICER WILLIAM MURDOCH: 40-50; a former Cockney who's taught himself to sound more educated; obedient to his superiors, he's nonetheless leery of the new technology and a little nervous about the *Titanic*.

ALICE FORTUNE: mid-20's, a no-nonsense turn-of-the-century feminist who also happens to be a knockout, she's the self-appointed warden to her less-than responsible baby brother, Charley.

CHARLEY FORTUNE: 19 and always on the move, he's convinced he'll be the next George M. Cohan; though caught between adolescence and adulthood, he's in no hurry to grow up.

THOMAS KILGANNON: early 20's and an outspoken Irish roughneck who knows his place in the social pecking order, he could not be less impressed by the aristocracy.

IDA STRAUS: mid-60's, elegant, and about fifty years ahead of her time, she adores her husband and plays the dutiful wife when necessary — yet we get a strong sense that she's the one who really wears the britches in the Straus home.

MARY CANAVAN: early 20's and charming, she's on her way to America to marry a man she's never met; not your typical colleen, she's independent and speaks her mind — much to Thomas' chagrin.

SETTING

The entire play takes place in the first-class smoking lounge of the R.M.S. *Titanic*, 350 miles southeast of Newfoundland, on the evening of April 14-15, 1912.

.ACT I   11:30 p.m.
ACT II   1:00 a.m.

Dedicated to

Charley Fortune, John Jacob Astor,
Isidor Straus, Ida Straus, William Murdoch,
Thomas Kilgannon, Mary Canavan,
and 1,496 others who never reached New York.

ACT I

(The lights come up full on the first-class smoking lounge of the R.M.S. Titanic, on the last night of her very brief life. The room, as would be expected, is decorated elegantly. Oak-paneled walls are separated at intervals by carefully cut stained glass windows, which in turn are flanked by elaborate gold and brass candelabras mounted on the casings and lit electrically. The carpets are thick; the hanging chandeliers are crystal. Throughout the room, we see several antique tables surrounded by stuffed chairs and love seats. There is a bar stage right and a door further down, which leads out onto the first-class deck. Along the stage left wall we see portholes; upstage center is a grand piano, situated next to another door.

At curtain rise, the room is empty. After a moment, the upstage door opens and JOHN JACOB ASTOR enters. He appears to be in his late forties and is dressed in black tie and tails. He crosses to the bar and pours himself a whisky; picking it up, he removes a gold watch from his pocket, checks the time, and glances expectantly at the door. With a slight head shake, he crosses to the center stage table and sits. After he has placed the drink beside him on the table, he withdraws from his jacket a deck of cards (which he also places on the table), and a pipe, which he proceeds to fill and light. While he is performing this chore, the upstage door opens again, and ISIDOR STRAUS enters stealthily. Appearing to be in his early sixties, he too is formally attired. ASTOR's back is to him so he is not aware that STRAUS has entered. ISIDOR moves quietly to the bar to mix himself a drink; ASTOR speaks without even looking up.)

ASTOR. You're late.

STRAUS. *(With slight Yiddish accent.)* Dammit, man—I am *not* late.

ASTOR. Eleven-thirty, Straus. We said eleven-thirty. That was eighteen seconds ago. Have you any idea how many shares can be traded in eighteen seconds?

STRAUS. That's the trouble with you industrialists. Tick-tick-tick-tick-tick-tick-tick. It's all you ever talk about. One would think you had some unholy alliance with the Swiss.

ASTOR. All right—

STRAUS. It is *not* all right. The human body is a delicate enough mechanism as is. If God had wanted us to be pocket watches, we'd have been born with Roman numerals. Where is the port?

ASTOR. The British drank it all.

STRAUS. Again? Good God, it's no wonder they lost the Revolution. I consider it an achievement of the highest order that they managed to find Philadelphia.

ASTOR. Boston.

STRAUS. You see? *(Pointing to ASTOR's glass.)* What are *you* having?

ASTOR. Whisky and soda.

STRAUS. You're no better.

(STRAUS begins pouring himself a sherry.)

ASTOR. Colonel Gracie was looking for you.

STRAUS. No doubt he was. And should he enquire again, I'd be most appreciative if you told him I'd fallen overboard.

ASTOR. Curious. I thought he was one of the few people you respected.

STRAUS. He was. Until he asked me to read his book. *The Truth About Chickamauga.* 462 pages. Never been so bored in my life.

ASTOR. I found it fascinating.

STRAUS. You exploit widows and children, too.

ASTOR. Mr. Straus, I consider that a highly inappropriate remark coming from a haberdasher.

STRAUS. My good man—one does not allude to Macy's with

the same sort of innuendo he might employ when speaking of some third-class necktie establishment. It reeks with envy. Do I make myself clear?

ASTOR. Perfectly. I'm sorry.

STRAUS. No, you're not. You're 47. You wear impertinence as though it were a two hundred dollar smoking jacket.

ASTOR. Yes. I know.

STRAUS. Well, you needn't be so smug about it.

ASTOR. I needn't? Arrogance is the cornerstone upon which every great empire is built. Without it, we should be destitute. *(Eyeing him.)* Evidently, some of us are.

(STRAUS crosses to the table and sits.)

STRAUS. Colonel Astor—practical hobby though they may well be, convertible debentures do not buy the same sense of security as a good piece of furniture.

ASTOR. Indeed. And how did you pay for passage on this vessel—with a davenport?

STRAUS. With the fruits gathered from forty years of hard labor. *(Pause.)* But I don't suppose you'd know about that, would you? You probably inherited the orchard, too.

ASTOR. There is nothing dishonorable in being born to the manor. A mere question of convenience, that's all. I was a fortunate soul.

STRAUS. You were a rich baby.

(ASTOR picks up the deck of cards.)

ASTOR. Deuces wild?

STRAUS. As always.

ASTOR. What about the stakes?

STRAUS. Might I interest you in raising them?

ASTOR. Of course.

STRAUS. Excellent. Three cents, then. *(From offstage, we hear ragtime music as ASTOR deals the cards. STRAUS groans.)* Oh, my God. There they go again.

ASTOR. I beg your pardon?

STRAUS. That band. They've been following me about this ship ever since we left Queenstown. I feel like the Pied Piper leading the rats to the sea.

ASTOR. Some people would consider that an honor.

STRAUS. Some people voted for Taft.

ASTOR. Speaking of rats.

STRAUS. My good fellow—I take it you dined this evening?

ASTOR. Of course. I had the squab.

STRAUS. I had the lamb. Rather, I *nearly* had the lamb.

ASTOR. I'll raise you.

STRAUS. Unfortunately, it is difficult to make oneself heard when the resident viola is attempting to play *Tales of Hoffmann* over one's shoulder. *(Pause.)* They gave me oysters. *(Pause.)* *Little* oysters. *(Pause.)* I abominate that band.

ASTOR. Oh, for God's sake, Straus. What did you expect on a first crossing—a selection labeled "silence"?

STRAUS. I didn't expect oysters.

ASTOR. Then you should have sailed the Lusitania.

STRAUS. Mrs. Straus wouldn't hear of it. It was either the Titanic or three more weeks of driving on the wrong side of the road. Given the alternatives, there didn't seem to be much of a choice.

ASTOR. Do you always do what your wife tells you?

STRAUS. Why not? She got lamb. *(Pause.)* Not that I'm complaining, mind you. This was supposed to be another honeymoon. Our fifth, I think.

ASTOR. Fifth?!

STRAUS. Blame Mrs. Straus. Whenever White Star launches another liner, she employs it as an excuse to reassemble her trousseau. One would think she held stock.

ASTOR. What has that to do with lamb?

STRAUS. Outside of the dining saloon, I haven't seen her since Friday.

ASTOR. She's been avoiding you?

STRAUS. She's been losing me. Colonel Astor—have you attempted to wander from one end of this ship to the other? It's like walking across New Jersey.

ASTOR. How can you quibble with technology? The Titanic has everything.
STRAUS. Yes. Including Articles of Statehood. I doubt that the forces of nature are much amused by the taunt.

(ASTOR pauses thoughtfully.)

ASTOR. You know, I envy you.
STRAUS. You should. Two pair.
ASTOR. Your marriage, I mean. There's something to be said for older spouses. They're devoted. They're reliable. They're—
STRAUS. Sturdy?
ASTOR. Well, yes.
STRAUS. My friend—one of these days you must allow me to point out the differences between an aging woman and a dented automobile.
ASTOR. I'd like to hear them.
STRAUS. No, you wouldn't. Don't patronize an old man.
ASTOR. I—
STRAUS. No need to apologize. Were I in your place, I wouldn't listen to me, either. Damn you.
ASTOR. She is lovely, isn't she?
STRAUS. At the very least.
ASTOR. My precious Kitty. I don't know what I would have done without her.
STRAUS. I didn't notice her in the dining saloon this evening. Is she feeling well?
ASTOR. Quite well. However, they've requested that I keep her in the cabin. She tends to bark around other people.
STRAUS. Your bride?!
ASTOR. Don't be a fool. My Airedale.
STRAUS. I was speaking of the new Mrs. Astor!
ASTOR. Oh. *(Pause.)* She's all right. A little seasick perhaps.
STRAUS. Colonel—pardon me for appearing inquisitive, but you don't seem to be entirely—
ASTOR. What? Bewitched? That sort of thing went out with McKinley.

STRAUS. Well, dammit, man—you might at least pretend. It's only polite.
ASTOR. Oh, come now, Straus. The second time out, a man is bound to be more cautious. Haven't you ever purchased a stock solely because it was expected to split? And then it didn't?
STRAUS. Occasionally.
ASTOR. There you are. Only a jackass would dive in twice with his eyes closed.
STRAUS. I see. (*Pause.*) Tell me—have you at least introduced yourselves to one another yet?
ASTOR. I hope so. She's pregnant.
STRAUS. The Airedale?!
ASTOR. My wife!
STRAUS. A wise choice. Three tens....

(*The upstage door opens and J. BRUCE ISMAY enters the lounge, looking quite a bit like the chairman of a steamship line. Probably because that's what he is.*)

ISMAY. Astor. Straus.
ASTOR. Oh, hello, Ismay.
ISMAY. I trust you'll ignore the intrusion. I didn't expect to find anyone playing cards on Sunday.

(*He begins surveying the room and taking notes on a small pad.*)

STRAUS. Preposterous. Why *shouldn't* anyone be playing cards on Sunday?
ASTOR. Don't be a heathen, Straus. Some people have morals.
STRAUS. And other people have money. It's a long-standing fact that the two cannot co-habit peacefully. Don't argue. It's been attempted many times.

(*ASTOR sees ISMAY's note-taking.*)

ASTOR. Bruce, what in God's name are you doing?
ISMAY. Planning a series of executions.

ASTOR. Come again?

ISMAY. The imbeciles who profess to understand the appointments of elegance. It's disgraceful. *(Indicating the lounge.)* I mean, really—who outside of the working class could possibly tolerate maroon and mauve in concert without wanting to vomit? This entire room looks like Macy's basement.

STRAUS. MR. ISMAY—

ISMAY. Consider it a compliment. *(Pointing toward the "B" deck.)* Assuming you'd like an education in *all* that's cheap, tasteless and vulgar, you might visit the Cafe Parisien. Wicker furniture, indeed. It gives one the distinct impression he's either in Hell or in America. *(To ASTOR.)* Do you think an aborigine carpet would complement the upholstery?

STRAUS. *(Mumbling.)* This man belongs in a sanitarium...

ASTOR. I really can't say that I've given the matter much thought.

ISMAY. Evidently, neither has anyone else. Too busy, I presume, wondering whether this leviathan would float in the first place.

ASTOR. I'd call that a reasonable concern.

ISMAY. You would. It's a sad comment upon the state of the human race when a man places the sanctity of life above offenses to the eye.

STRAUS. If I were you, I'd be more concerned about what's offensive to the ear. That band, for instance.

ISMAY. Indeed. Have you a suggestion?

STRAUS. Personally, I'd recommend poison.

ISMAY. I beg your pardon?

ASTOR. Never mind him. He's under the weather.

STRAUS. You would be too if you hadn't eaten since noon. *(Mumbling.)* Oysters....

ISMAY. Well, should it make you feel any better, we expect to be in New York two hours ahead of schedule. Isn't that excellent news?

STRAUS. Tick-tick-tick-tick-tick-tick-tick. *(Pause.)* Ecch.

ISMAY. I say—have I said something wrong?

ASTOR. Not at all. Have a drink.

ISMAY. I really can't—

ASTOR. I don't know why not. White Star is paying for it.

STRAUS. Oh, leave the poor man alone, Astor. Can't you see you've just cost him half a minute?

ASTOR. Straus—

STRAUS. You heard him. We've gained two hours already.

ASTOR. Really, that's quite enough—

STRAUS. Left to his own devices, he'll have us arriving in New York three days before we left England. *(To ISMAY.)* Why don't you retire to bed with a good book? I have one about Chickamauga I'd be happy to inflict upon you—

ISMAY. Dear God—that candelabra is crooked! If I find the idiot who did that—

ASTOR. Have a drink, Bruce.

ISMAY. Perhaps I will.

(He crosses to the bar and begins mixing himself a drink.)

STRAUS. Just don't go looking for the port. Your countrymen got there first.

ASTOR. Ismay, do you mind if I make a suggestion?

ISMAY. About the carpet?

ASTOR. Not about the carpet! *(Pause.)* You might consider going a bit more lightly on yourself. Anxiety doesn't befit a chairman of the board.

ISMAY. I suppose you presume mine is an enviable lot?

ASTOR. You could do a great deal worse.

ISMAY. I could do a great deal better, too. Would you like a reasonable example? Mr. Guggenheim's eggs were undercooked and I forgot to apologize. What kind of a life is that? If I — *(Looking down, then mumbling.)* Dammit, we're out of ice.

STRAUS. I wouldn't concern myself too much were I you. Mr. *Guggenheim* is undercooked.

ASTOR. He speaks quite highly of *you.*

STRAUS. That's because he's a born liar.

ASTOR. Aren't we all?

STRAUS. My point exactly. He's not very good at it yet. It often happens to those who still belong to the middle classes.

ASTOR. Really, Straus. A man who has a million dollars is as well off as if he were rich.

STRAUS. Well, there goes Guggenheim's last excuse.

(ISMAY sits at the table with his drink. As he does, the chandelier begins to sway noticeably above them. They do not see it. After a moment, it stops.)

ISMAY. Another headache I don't need. Have you seen our passenger manifest? It looks like the Social Register.

ASTOR. Not quite. J. P. Morgan isn't here.

STRAUS. Immaterial. J. P. Morgan's presence is of no commercial value to the White Star Line.

ASTOR. Why is that?

ISMAY and STRAUS. He *owns* the White Star Line.

ASTOR. Odd. I thought *I* did.

STRAUS. Who balances your checkbook?

ASTOR. *(To ISMAY.)* You know, it's your own fault. You needn't have touted the launching of this ship as though it were the Second Coming of Christ. Ismay, it's only a boat.

ISMAY. If the Titanic is only a boat, then you, Astor, are only a banker.

STRAUS. Hear, hear.

ASTOR. Perhaps you ought to come work for me, Bruce. I like your style.

STRAUS. I don't. Personally, I find it unnatural crossing the sea on a vessel with its own coastline. Forgive me. I'm unusual that way. *(To ASTOR.)* I'll raise you.

ASTOR. I think you're bluffing.

STRAUS. Prove it. *(They turn over their cards.)* Damn!

ASTOR. You owe me a dime. *(Looks up suddenly.)* Are we slowing down?

STRAUS. *(Indicating ISMAY.)* For God's sake, Astor. Don't get him started.

ISMAY. I shouldn't be surprised if we were. Captain Smith pilots this ship as though it were a leaky tug. Evidently seventy revolutions is more than the old bird can handle.

STRAUS. Which old bird? The leaky tug or Captain Smith?

ISMAY. Is there a discernible difference? I should consider firing him if he weren't already retiring. He thinks it was his idea. *(Pause; looking about, worried.)* We *are* slowing down. *(A grumble.)* Dammit, I told him not to take those warnings seriously. This is the Titanic, for God's sake.

ASTOR. What warnings?

ISMAY. Nothing we need worry about. Leave that to the poor wretches on the Carpathia. Damn Cunarder.

(The down right door opens. FIRST OFFICER WILLIAM MURDOCH enters, slightly out of breath. He crosses to ISMAY.)

MURDOCH. Mr. Ismay—

ISMAY. Murdoch! Why aren't you in the wheelhouse? Who's at the helm?

MURDOCH. Lightoller's taken over, sir. There's been a bit of trouble. Captain Smith would like to see you on the bridge.

ISMAY. Just what I need.

STRAUS. I doubt it's anything serious. While you're there, why don't you have the ship's railing repainted peach?

ISMAY. Astor, what time is it?

ASTOR.. *(Checking his watch.)* Eleven-fifty.

ISMAY. Too late to go groveling before Mr. Guggenheim. *(A shrug.)* Oh, well. Something to look forward to tomorrow. The senile old buffoon.

ASTOR. Bruce, what do you say about *us* when our backs are turned?

ISMAY. Nothing you'd want to hear.

STRAUS. *(To ASTOR.)* At least he's honest.

(ISMAY crosses to MURDOCH.)

ISMAY. What seems to be the problem?

(MURDOCH mumbles into ISMAY's ear.)

ISMAY. WHAT? YOU FOOL!
MURDOCH. Begging your pardon, sir. I was only following orders—

(ISMAY tears out of the room, with MURDOCH close behind. ASTOR turns to STRAUS.)

ASTOR. You know, you were damned rude. Ismay looks like a decent fellow.
STRAUS. He looks like an undertaker.
ASTOR. What if he does? That's no excuse for uncivilized behavior.
STRAUS. It's not? We're entrusting our lives to a man with a mouth full of carpet tacks, and you're talking to me about uncivilized behavior?
ASTOR. Oh, for God's sake, Straus. Why do you bother to travel at all?
STRAUS. Can't be helped. I just purchased land over there. The Missus insisted.
ASTOR. Really? I'm considering buying some European property myself. Just got through picking it out, as a matter of fact.
STRAUS. Good investment. Mine goes by the name of Tunbridge Wells. What's yours called?
ASTOR. Spain.
STRAUS. Deal the cards.

(The downstage door opens suddenly, and ALICE FORTUNE enters looking severely agitated. She's just this side of 25 and a real pip, dressed in a pale blue evening gown and long white gloves. Without breaking stride, she begins circling the room and calling out as she does.)

ALICE. Charles! I'm speaking to you, Charles! Are you in here? *(Pause.)* Answer me!

(STRAUS looks up.)

STRAUS. Young woman, should you find it necessary to bray further in this direction, kindly provide some sort of advance notice. One generally requires lead time to seek appropriate shelter.

ALICE. Have you seen my brother?

STRAUS. Happily, that is one hardship I have been spared. On the whole, I think I'd prefer a bullet wound.

ASTOR. Indeed. *(To ALICE.)* I must say, this intrusion of yours is typically inconsiderate. One would presume you'd learned by now that this is a male sanctuary. *(Pause.)* Or do you consider trespass another of your misplaced prerogatives?

ALICE. Sergeant Astor—

ASTOR. "Colonel."

ALICE. I assure you I have no interest in interrupting the exchange of rude post cards or whatever it is that you do in here. I am simply looking for my baby brother. My gentle, sensitive, defenseless baby brother. And if I find him, I'm going to break him in half.

ASTOR. Is that a promise or merely an idle threat?

ALICE. A blood oath.

(STRAUS and ASTOR glance at one other, then put down their cards and rise.)

ASTOR. I'll check the "A" deck.

STRAUS. I'll look in the cafe.

ALICE. Don't bother. *(She faces front and calls out again.)* Charles, I'm going to give you one more chance. Do you hear me? *(Pause.)* I'm warning you, Charles.

ASTOR. Oh, for God's sake. Anyone can see that he isn't here.

STRAUS. *(To ASTOR.)* Don't antagonize her, Astor. Clearly the woman has gone mad.

ALICE. Have I? *(Singing.)* "H-A-double R-I, G-A-N spells Harrigan—"

(Suddenly, from behind the bar, we hear a strong young

baritone voice responding helplessly on cue.)

VOICE. *(Singing.)* "Proud of all the Irish blood that's in me, Divil a man can say a word agin me—"

(ASTOR turns to STRAUS.)

ASTOR. Dammit. I was hoping he'd fallen over the railing.
VOICE. "H-A-double R-I, G-A-N, you see—"

(ALICE crosses upstage impatiently, folds her arms as she reaches the bar, and addresses herself to the area behind it.)

ALICE. Charles Alexander Fortune, you come out of there this instant.

(CHARLEY FORTUNE rises slowly. About 19 and blond, with a couple thousand real white teeth, he's dressed in a gray, three-piece suit with a red-and-white striped vest and a blue bow tie with white dots. He looks like Betsy Ross. He's also wearing a straw boater and carrying a song-and-dance man's cane.)

CHARLEY. "It's a name that a shame never has been connected with, Harrigan—that's me." *(To ALICE.)* Don't ever do that again.
ALICE. Oh, Charles—how could you?
CHARLEY. How could I what?
ALICE. Don't play games with me, Charles. You're not too old for—
STRAUS. —fratricide?
ASTOR. Indeed.
CHARLEY. *(To ALICE.)* It seemed like a funny idea. A cute little boyish prank. Don't you think I'm cute anymore, Alice? *(Pause; pointing.)* I still have a dimple. *(Acid silence.)* Alice? *(Pause.)* WELL, WHO KNEW HE'D SAY YES?!
ALICE. Where is it?
CHARLEY. Where is what?
ALICE. The Marconigram.

CHARLEY. Who said I got a Marconigram?
ALICE. Mother.
CHARLEY. Whose mother?
ALICE. Stand still, Charles. It's difficult to hit a moving target.
CHARLEY. I lost it. Okay?
ALICE. Then what are you hiding?
CHARLEY. Nothing. A dinner menu.

(She grabs it from behind his back and scans it.)

ALICE. From George M. Cohan?

(STRAUS turns to ASTOR.)

STRAUS. I wonder if *he* got oysters.

(ALICE looks up and indicates the telegram.)

ALICE. Oh, Charles, how could you? What am I going to tell them back home?

(CHARLEY races to the piano and begins accompanying himself.)

CHARLEY. *(Singing.)* "Say hello to dear old Coney Isle if there you chance to be, When you're at the Waldorf have a smile and charge it up to me—"
ALICE. Why must you do that?
CHARLEY. Because I'm the original cranky Yankee popular melody fool.
ALICE. If you're looking for an argument, it's going to be a long wait.
CHARLEY. Alice—
ALICE. *(Waving the telegram.)* Go ahead! Say yes! I'd like to see you live on twenty-five dollars a week.
CHARLEY. I can afford it. I have very simple tastes.
ALICE. Since when? *(Eyeing his clothes.)* That suit didn't

exactly come from Macy's, you know.
STRAUS. *(To ASTOR.)* Might I borrow a shotgun?

(CHARLEY grabs a chair and sits at the table with ASTOR and STRAUS.)

CHARLEY. Guess what?
ASTOR. You're having your larynx removed.
CHARLEY. No, no—I'm serious.
STRAUS. As though he weren't? *(Handing him the deck.)* It's your deal.
ASTOR. *(To STRAUS.)* Must you?
STRAUS. Colonel Astor, preferential though your company may be, the fact of the matter remains that you win. He doesn't. *(To CHARLEY.)* The cards please, Mr. Fortune.
CHARLEY. *(Dealing.)* It's called *Broadway Jones*. We go into rehearsal in September—
ALICE. We do *not* go into rehearsal in September—because the season won't be over yet—
CHARLEY. Aw, who cares about pitching?
ALICE. Don't talk like that. And as to my appearing in public in a bustle, I'd just as soon swim back to New York.
ASTOR. That's an excellent idea—
ALICE. Who asked you? *(To CHARLEY; indicating the telegram.)* Besides, this only says "audition"—
STRAUS. *(To ASTOR.)* I'll raise you.
ASTOR. I'm out.

(From outside, we hear a distant shouting. ASTOR rises, disturbed, and begins crossing to the window. Halfway there, he changes his mind and heads for the bar instead, where he proceeds to mix himself a drink.)

CHARLEY. *(To ALICE.)* Sis, I'm telling you—we're as good as in. Why else would he remember us? And after three whole years?
ALICE. Why else, indeed. Charles, in case it hasn't yet penetrated your skull, which is a challenging dig at the best of times,

an amateur contest at Lake Tonawanda hardly puts one in the same class as Fay Templeton and Eddie Foy. Unless this Mr. Cohan thinks we're just a couple of Canadian rubes who can be had for a song—
CHARLEY. Song! We'll do "Push Me Along in My Pushcart", and—
ALICE. We'll do nothing of the kind. If Harriet Blatch ever finds out about this, she'll have my corset revoked. *(To STRAUS.)* Excuse me.
STRAUS. It's much too late for that.
CHARLEY. Harriet Blatch is a fat old cow.
ALICE. How can you say that about a pioneer?!
CHARLEY. No! No! Davy Crockett was a pioneer.
ALICE. It's the same thing!
CHARLEY. EXCEPT DAVY CROCKETT WAS A LOT PRETTIER THAN HARRIET BLATCH IS!
STRAUS. *(Mumbling.)* I wish I were deaf. *(To CHARLEY.)* I'll raise you.

(ALICE peers over CHARLEY's shoulder at his poker hand.)

ALICE. Play the king, you idiot.
CHARLEY. Which one?
STRAUS. *(Throwing in his cards.)* Never mind, never mind.

(ASTOR, standing at the window, frowns.)

ASTOR. What the devil is going on out there?
ALICE. *(Looking up.)* I think we passed a berg of some sort. There's ice all over the forward deck.
STRAUS. An iceberg, did you say?
ASTOR. *(Peering out the window.)* Apparently.
STRAUS. Well, for God's sake, don't tell Ismay. He'll probably want to decorate it.

(ASTOR returns to his seat.)

CHARLEY. *(To ALICE.)* Would you please get your hands off

my cards?

ALICE. Suit yourself. I'm not going to waste my time arguing with a child.

CHARLEY. Great Honk, Alice! I'm almost 20.

ALICE. Indeed? Well, they have this thing called adolescence. You might consider passing through it—

CHARLEY. Oh, yeah? Why don't you go burn a girdle or somethin'?

ALICE. Why don't you go outside and play with the anchor?

CHARLEY. How'd you like to make me?

ALICE. How'd you like a split lip?

CHARLEY. *(Slamming down his cards.)* Full house.

ALICE. *(Ditto.)* Royal flush.

CHARLEY. I'm going back to my cabin.

ALICE. Have you considered the Bluejackets, Charley? They think they're going to win another pennant. What do you plan to tell them— that their right-handed ace decided to shuffle off to Buffalo instead?

CHARLEY. Why don't you ask Harriet Blatch?

ALICE. I don't have to. You know what she'd say?

CHARLEY. Yeah. "Moo."

ALICE. God, I hope you were adopted!

CHARLEY. Look who's talkin'. Know what your trouble is, Sis? Next to Pop, *I'm* supposed to be the man in this family. Not you. What happens if I get bigger than Cohan? Can you hear my curtain speech? "My mother thanks you, my father thanks you, my sister Ethel thanks you, my sister Mabel thanks you—and then there's my brother. Alice."

ALICE. I will *not* become a Floradora girl just so you can give your regards to Broadway!

CHARLEY. *(Rising.)* ARE YOU GONNA DO THE AUDITION WITH ME OR NOT?!

ALICE. *(Also rising.)* I'LL CONSIDER IT!

(They sit. ALICE picks up the deck and begins shuffling furiously. ASTOR turns to STRAUS and points to CHARLEY.)

ASTOR. I see no earthly use for that boy, do you?

(STRAUS indicates CHARLEY's vest and tie.)

STRAUS. Oh, I don't know. If he'd been born fifty years earlier, they could have flown him over Ft. Sumter.

(As ALICE begins to deal the cards, the upstage door opens slowly, and we see THOMAS KILGANNON peering cautiously into the room. His tousled hair and ruddy complexion clearly indicate that he is Irish—his worn trousers and faded blue jumper are just as much of a tip-off that he is a peasant. When he sees that ASTOR, STRAUS, CHARLEY and ALICE are seated downstage with their backs to him, he quickly reaches behind the partially opened door and pulls an obviously reluctant woman into the room with him. She too is dressed poorly; her skirt is somewhat tattered and a shawl is draped over her head, covering her face as well. We also notice that THOMAS' pants—from the knees down—are drenched with sea water. Apparently oblivious to this, he tightens his grip on the woman's arm, motions her to be silent, and propels her toward the down right door leading out to the boat deck, where they exit quickly. No one at the card table has been aware of their presence.)

ASTOR. *(To ALICE.)* Miss Fortune—

ALICE. Don't call me that. You make me sound like Calamity Jane.

ASTOR. Haven't you a riot you could be instigating elsewhere on this ship?

ALICE. Are you attempting to get rid of me?

ASTOR. Strenuously.

ALICE. I wouldn't hold my breath.

ASTOR. In that event, I think we'd all be most appreciative if you would permit someone else to deal those cards.

ALICE. Why is that? Do I threaten your manhood?

ASTOR. You cheat.

ALICE. Really, Lieutenant—

ASTOR. "Colonel."

ALICE. There is, after all, a major distinction between a victor and a thief—

ASTOR. I'm aware of that—

ALICE. —and I resent the innuendo that, simply because I don't happen to be male, I am incapable of succeeding honestly—

STRAUS. Young woman, I don't believe that's what he was implying.

ASTOR. It certainly was.

ALICE. Not that it's any of your business, but I can shuffle a deck and chalk a billiard cue at the same time—

ASTOR. Cunning achievement—

ALICE. So you'll forgive me if I find your attitude, at best, despicable.

CHARLEY. *(Under his breath.)* Alice, shut up.

STRAUS. *(To ASTOR.)* Really, Colonel Astor—I believe an apology is in order.

ALICE. *(To CHARLEY; under her breath.)* I *won't* shut up—

ASTOR. *(To STRAUS.)* Are you mad? A billiard cue? What kind of accomplishment is that?

CHARLEY. *(To ALICE; gritted teeth.)* Then change the subject—

STRAUS. *(To ASTOR.)* Can *you* do it?

ASTOR. That's immaterial.

ALICE. *(To CHARLEY.)* I *won't* change the subject. I'm making a point!

CHARLEY. *(Sotto voce.)* No, you're not! You just dealt me five aces!

(CHARLEY passes ALICE the fifth ace under the table. She slips him a new card, then sticks the ace in her shoe.)

ASTOR. Oh, all right! I apologize!

ALICE. I should hope you would.

ASTOR. *(To STRAUS; mumbling.)* Really, I have half a mind—

ALICE. You needn't brag about it.

ASTOR.—to lodge a formal protest.

STRAUS. *(Indicating ALICE.)* With whom? The steamship line or God?

ASTOR. If White Star persists in allowing persons such as these to upset the equilibrium of the caste system, there's no telling what might happen. Can you imagine the consequences? Public flesh displays in Herald Square! Intransigent dismissal of the law! If—

(ALICE looks up suddenly.)

ALICE. Why have we stopped?
CHARLEY. *(To ALICE.)* Sshhh! I want to hear the rest of this. *(To ASTOR.)* Go back to the part about public flesh displays.
ALICE. Charley, we're not moving!
STRAUS. Preposterous.

(ASTOR cocks his head.)

ASTOR. I do believe she's right.
STRAUS. *You* believe *she's* right?
ASTOR. This is the Twentieth Century. Anything is possible.
CHARLEY. But in the middle of the ocean?
STRAUS. It only looks that way. Perhaps the front end of the ship just docked in New York.
ASTOR. Listen. *(Pause.)* They've shut down the turbines.

(They all strain.)

ALICE. I don't hear anything.

(From offstage, MRS. STRAUS. Like her husband, she speaks with a slight Yiddish accent.)

MRS. STRAUS' VOICE. ISIDOR!
STRAUS. I do. *(Rising hastily.)* Is there a back way out of here?

(Before he can move, the side door opens and MRS. STRAUS enters. She is in her early sixties and formidable, and is presently followed by OFFICER MURDOCH, who is holding onto a rather cumbersome-looking lifejacket.)

MURDOCH. Ma'am, it's for your own protection!

MRS. STRAUS. I won't hear of it! Surely you can find someone else to protect!

MURDOCH. You have my word they're quite comfortable.

MRS. STRAUS. Young man, those who wear burlap with pearls deserve whatever happens to them. Why, it's—it's ludicrous!

(MURDOCH turns to STRAUS.)

MURDOCH. Mr. Straus, sir—if you might attempt a word with your wife—

STRAUS. What do you think I've been doing for forty years?

MRS. STRAUS. Thirty-nine—

STRAUS. You see? She wasn't always like this. She gets it from my daughter.

MRS. STRAUS. *My* daughter—

STRAUS. Ida, don't start. Not here.

MRS. STRAUS. How can you call yourself a father—

STRAUS. —the North Atlantic is no place for—

MRS. STRAUS.—letting her marry that—that thing!

STRAUS. ALFRED HESS IS A GOOD MAN!

MRS. STRAUS. He's nothing of the kind. He's a rum-runner.

STRAUS. —a diligent, hardworking soul—

MRS. STRAUS. —a pirate—

STRAUS. —who will some day leave an indelible mark on the world—

MRS. STRAUS. —by selling little children to the Chinese, no doubt.

(The downstage door leading toward the boat deck opens slowly; once again, we see THOMAS KILGANNON peering carefully into the lounge, apparently hoping to retrace his earlier steps and make it back across the room and out through the upstage door. When he sees the other six characters downstage with their backs to him, he realizes he's going to have to take this one by degrees; darting into the lounge silently, he ducks behind the bar before the others have a chance to turn and see

him. As he does so, we notice that the Irish woman whom he accompanied earlier is no longer with him; we also observe that THOMAS is barechested and shivering. In the meantime, ASTOR has risen and approached MURDOCH.)

ASTOR. Officer, what is this all about?

(MRS. STRAUS interrupts.)

MRS. STRAUS. Haven't you heard? There's the nastiest rumor floating around this ship—
ASTOR. *(To himself.)* Disturbing choice of words—
MRS. STRAUS. Of course, I really shouldn't be repeating it, as the source was hardly reliable—
MURDOCH. Mrs. Straus—
MRS. STRAUS. All right, Mrs. J. J. Brown, if you must know. From Denver. Wherever *that* is—
STRAUS. Ida—
MRS. STRAUS. Oh, she's really quite common. All got up in green and gold, she looks like a Christmas tree. Wears emeralds, too, if you can believe that. In April—
MURDOCH. Ma'am, I have my orders to think about—
ALICE. *(Rising.)* Mrs. Straus—
MRS. STRAUS. Oh, hello, dear. What a lovely gown. Where did you get it—Gimbels?
STRAUS. IDA!
MRS. STRAUS. Yes, well it seems that Mrs. Brown was on her way to the cafe when she slipped and fell, of all things, on this piece of ice, and—
ALICE. Oh, my God. Where?
MRS. STRAUS. On her rear end, I'm afraid. Made the most dreadful noises and then—
MURDOCH. Mrs. Straus! SHUT UP!

(A shocked silence. MRS. STRAUS turns to her husband.)

MRS. STRAUS. Isidor! Are you going to let him talk to me that

way?
STRAUS. Yes.

(Upstage, THOMAS darts out silently from behind the bar, and races across twelve feet of carpet before sliding headfirst into a hidden corner behind the piano.)

MURDOCH. *(To MRS. STRAUS.)* Forgive me, Ma'am. *(Indicating the lifejacket.)* But if you know what's good for you, you'll put this on. *(To the others.)* And it wouldn't be entirely unwise if the rest of you did the same.

(ALICE reaches out for her brother.)

ALICE. Charley?
CHARLEY. *(Rising.)* Officer, I think you'd better tell us what's happened to the ship.
MURDOCH. I'll tell you what's happened. There's a great big bloody— *(Flustered over the profanity.)* Uh—that is—

(ISMAY appears in the doorway.)

ISMAY. Murdoch! What are you doing in here?!
MURDOCH. I'm attempting to do my job, sir. That which His Majesty's Navy and the International Mercantile Marine employs me to—
ISMAY. Indeed? And I presume that includes your impeccable navigational skills?
MURDOCH. If I may say so, sir—
ISMAY. You may *not* say so, you incompetent halfwit.
ASTOR. Really, Bruce—if something's gone wrong, I do believe we're entitled to hear it. At least with enough notice to sell any stock we have in this damned line.
ISMAY. What makes you think anything's gone wrong?
ASTOR. Oh, I don't know. Just a hunch. Half the ship appears to be buried under a ton of ice, all the engines are off, and if I'm not mistaken, we're listing five degrees to port!

ISMAY. Besides that—

ASTOR. Now, see here, Ismay—

ISMAY. A slight scrape, that's all. Why, if it weren't for the photographers waiting in New York harbor, we shouldn't even have stopped to investigate.

MURDOCH. Sir—

ISMAY. *(Picking up the lifejacket.)* And I can assure you there'll be no need for these. God himself could not sink this ship.

STRAUS. Yes, well, have any of your people *checked* with God lately? He may have given you an old itinerary.

(MURDOCH points toward the boat deck as ASTOR slips out the side door.)

MURDOCH. He's right, Mr. Ismay. They've already uncovered the—

(ISMAY grinds a heel into MURDOCH's foot and turns to CHARLEY.)

ISMAY. You'll forgive the poor fellow, Mr. Cohan. He's clearly not cut out for this line of work.

MURDOCH. I'm a British seaman, sir.

ISMAY. "Were" a British seaman, Murdoch. I'll see to the change in tenses once we reach port.

MURDOCH. "If", sir.

ISMAY. Get out.

MRS. STRAUS. Just a moment. *(She steps forward and puts a hand on MURDOCH's arm.)* This charming young man was kind enough to offer his assistance when a dear, dear friend sustained an injury to her—to her— Well, at any rate, I'm afraid I was the one behaving frightfully. *(To STRAUS.)* Wasn't I?

STRAUS. Always.

(MRS. STRAUS picks up the lifejacket and addresses MURDOCH.)

MRS. STRAUS. It really looks like quite a clever device after

all. What is it?
MURDOCH. A lifejacket, Ma'am.
MRS. STRAUS. How—how useful. Tell me, Mr. Murdoch. Do you suppose you could find one in a pale blue? With perhaps a thin silver trim?
MURDOCH. *(Quietly.)* Thank you, Mrs. Straus.

(He heads for the upstage door.)

    ISMAY. Murdoch?
    MURDOCH. Sir?
    ISMAY. You're an imbecile.
    MURDOCH. Of course, sir.

(He leaves. At the same time, THOMAS peers out from behind the piano, sees that the others are turned toward MURDOCH by the down right door, and so quickly rises and makes his break through the upstage exit. Then he, too, is gone. After a moment, MRS. STRAUS gingerly picks up the lifejacket with distaste and drops it unceremoniously behind the bar, as her husband turns to ISMAY and indicates MURDOCH's exit.)

    STRAUS. Have a high turnover rate, do you?
    ISMAY. Strangely, yes. I've often wondered why. Perhaps it's because their crania are smaller than ours. They don't have much of an attention span, you know.
    STRAUS. Tell me—have you ever considered treating them fairly?
    ISMAY. No. But I despise them equally. Propriety demands it.
    STRAUS. I see. Sorry if I misjudged you.
    ISMAY. Not at all. Good evening.

(He exits. There's a reflective silence.)

    MRS. STRAUS. That man is a pain in the—
    STRAUS. Ida, please.
    MRS. STRAUS. —neck.

(She sits and begins helping her husband lay down a solitaire hand. CHARLEY rises hastily and fakes a yawn.)

CHARLEY. Gosh, it's late. I think I'll go back to my cabin and see about getting' some—

(—except ALICE is blocking the upstage door.)

CHARLEY. (Mumbling.) Uh-oh.
ALICE. Charley?
CHARLEY. What?

(She begins backing him to the wall.)

ALICE. Come here.
CHARLEY. No.
ALICE. Charles—
CHARLEY. I don't wanna. Stay where you are.
ALICE. Why did he call you "Mr. Cohan"?
CHARLEY. Slip of the tongue?
ALICE. You'll have to do better than that.
CHARLEY. Uh—maybe he recognized a Broadway Kid when he saw one. *(Fast time step.) You* know—my famous walk, my fancy talk, my happy grin, my—ALICE, IF YOU SOCK ME IN FRONT OF OTHER PEOPLE, I SWEAR I'M GONNA—
ALICE. What did you tell him?
CHARLEY. Nothing! Honest! I didn't say a word! He heard it from Lady Duff Gordon.
ALICE. And where did *she* get it?
CHARLEY. From the Countess of Rothes. She heard it from Guggenheim who musta got it from Major Butt, who, let's see, I guess heard it from Captain Smith. OKAY?
ALICE. Why does Captain Smith think you're George M. Cohan?
CHARLEY. Him I told.
ALICE. And he believed you?
CHARLEY. He had to. I gave him passes to opening night.

Broadway Jones? We go into rehearsal in September—
ALICE. That's disgraceful.
CHARLEY. Yeah, well, you haven't heard the half of it yet. I told him they were from you, too—
ALICE. From me?!?
CHARLEY. Well, not you exactly. From George's sister. Josie. *(Pause.)* My co-star? *(Pause.)* Whom I love? *(Pause.)* Dearly?
ALICE. Do you have any last requests?
CHARLEY. Yeah. Don't bust anything higher than the chin. My face is my future....

(They continue their argument in pantomime as the lights dim slightly on them. At the downstage table, STRAUS looks up from his solitaire game and indicates CHARLEY.)

STRAUS. And you complain about Alfred Hess. Your daughter could be married to *that*.
MRS. STRAUS. It's no worse than being married to Long John Silver. *(Kibitzing.)* Red eight under black nine.
STRAUS. Come now, Ida. You make him sound as though he wore a gold earring, went about visibly unshaven, and had rotting teeth.

(A beat.)

MRS. STRAUS. I never said he wore a gold earring.
STRAUS. He's a decent provider.
MRS. STRAUS. Granted.
STRAUS. He seems to love her a great deal.
MRS. STRAUS. I'm not denying that.
STRAUS. What, then?
MRS. STRAUS. Isidor, every young woman has the right to be treated, however briefly, as though she were a princess. *(Pause.)* It's a practice that's been going on for years.
STRAUS. So I recall.
MRS. STRAUS. Of course, some are luckier than others. They never learn of the deception. *(Pause.)* Alfred Hess, on the other hand,

behaves as if he married a—a—
STRAUS. Wife?
MRS. STRAUS. In so many words.
STRAUS. Perhaps that's what she wants.
MRS. STRAUS. Oh, she's much too young to know what she wants. Common sense is a late-blooming fruit—and regrettably, by the time it's ripe enough to pick, most people have already died. Take that poor child who married your Colonel Astor. For her sake, I do hope she's never kidnapped for ransom.
STRAUS. I beg your pardon?
MRS. STRAUS. Can you see what would happen if he were asked to provide a description? He'd have to refer the authorities to someone who actually knew her. *(Pause.)* I can't quite imagine them in nightclothes, can you? He probably makes her salute.
STRAUS. I don't see where Alfred Hess—
MRS. STRAUS. Alfred Hess took our child to France on something they called a honeymoon. And what does she still talk about to this day?
STRAUS. Paris.
MRS. STRAUS. Exactly. Nothing more.
STRAUS. Maybe she enjoyed herself. She certainly spent enough.
MRS. STRAUS. Rubbish. I've enjoyed myself as well. And I don't believe I've *ever* seen Paris.
STRAUS. Don't be a fool. I've taken you there at least six times.
MRS. STRAUS. Seven. And all I remember is that enchanting little cafe on the Rue Cambon—
STRAUS. Yes, well, that's quite enough.
MRS. STRAUS. I'm sure it isn't. Really, Mr. Straus. If you didn't understand the language, there was no shame in admitting it.
STRAUS. Madam, I speak French as well as any native!
MRS. STRAUS. Don't raise your voice, Isidor.
STRAUS. Then don't accuse me.
MRS. STRAUS. One would hardly call it an accusation.
STRAUS. I don't wish to discuss this.
MRS. STRAUS. Did you or did you not order veal?
STRAUS. That I did.

MRS. STRAUS. And did they or did they not bring us monkey?
STRAUS. The waiter was deaf.
MRS. STRAUS. He most certainly was not. He heard me scream.
STRAUS. And your sensibilities are that much more indigenous to the Continent than mine? I seem to recall the Louvre—
MRS. STRAUS. Robbery. Pure and simple. At best, I consider it highly questionable that the French require the use of that ridiculous-looking currency in the first place—much less to view damaged works of art.
STRAUS. That statue was not damaged.
MRS. STRAUS. How can you say that? Her arms had fallen off.
STRAUS. She wasn't *supposed* to have arms.
MRS. STRAUS. That was *their* story.
STRAUS. You're missing the point! *(Pause.)* I think in the future you might be a bit more solicitous of Alfred Hess. Don't you?
MRS. STRAUS. I'll consider it.
STRAUS. I'm quite serious, Ida.
MRS. STRAUS. So am I. And if it should make you happy, I'll send him a gift. A small one. Will that be sufficient?
STRAUS. That's extremely generous of you, my dear. What sort of gift did you have in mind?
MRS. STRAUS. Fifteen men on a dead man's chest. *(Pause.)* Yo-ho-ho and a bottle of—
STRAUS. You exasperate me.
MRS. STRAUS. I practice.

(STRAUS puts down his cards and speaks carefully.)

STRAUS. Ida—depending upon whether one subscribes to Mr. Ismay or Mrs. Brown, it is conceivable that we may not be returning to Paris again.
MRS. STRAUS. Yes. I know.
STRAUS. Then I feel it only fair to warn you. Whatever the verdict, I shall not tolerate any heroics.
MRS. STRAUS. And neither shall I. *(Looking down.)* Black two under red three.

STRAUS. Really, Madam. They call it "solitaire."
MRS. STRAUS. They do? How foolish....

(The lights come up full again on CHARLEY and ALICE.)

CHARLEY. Okay—what was I supposed to tell them?
ALICE. The truth might have been a cleansing novelty.
CHARLEY. The truth about what? Pitching for the Winnipeg Bluejackets? Oh, boy, Alice. That would have gone over real big in the first-class dining saloon. They'd have had me finishing my creamed carrots in steerage.
ALICE. Don't be silly. Father would never let that happen.
CHARLEY. Father would have been holding the door open! Sis, are your ears broken? I hate it! I hate the uniforms and I hate the crowds and most of all I hate—
ALICE. Charley, we decided—
CHARLEY. No! No! *You* decided. I lost my right to free speech the day you gave it to Harriet Blatch.
ALICE. What has *she* got to do with it?
CHARLEY. Alice, you used to *want* to dance with me. I mean, wasn't that the whole idea? I didn't know it was exploitation—I thought it was a time step. *(Pause.)* You just—well, you—you picked her over your own brother, didn't you?
ALICE. Oh, Charley! Do you really believe that?
CHARLEY. Well, that's the way it looks. What the heck do you think I'm trying to get us to 42nd Street for? To keep Congress from giving you the vote? For Pete's sake, Alice—I don't care about equal rights. I don't even care about all that Yankee Doodle stuff. Much. *(Looking down.)* I— I just want my sister back.

(There's a pause. ALICE puts a hand to his cheek.)

ALICE. Charles, sometimes you can be such a—such a boy.
CHARLEY. I'm allowed.
ALICE. You don't have to pretend you're George M. Cohan or anybody else. Not for me. Not ever.
CHARLEY. Then would you—would you do the audition with

me? Please? Even if it means breaking a couple dumb rules?
ALICE. What about the Bluejackets?
CHARLEY. Yeah. What about them?
ALICE. I thought it was a good idea, Charley. But if you dislike it that much, just say so.
CHARLEY. You mean it? You'll really listen?
ALICE. I didn't know it would make you this unhappy.
CHARLEY. And you won't get angry?
ALICE. I promise.
CHARLEY. Alice?
ALICE. What?
CHARLEY. I don't want you to pitch anymore.
ALICE. That's too bad.
CHARLEY. I thought you said you would listen!
ALICE. I did listen. Now you listen to *me*. What am I going to tell the Countess of Rhodes—
CHARLEY. —Rothes—
ALICE. —when she asks me what *Broadway Jones* is about? That I've got amnesia?
CHARLEY. *I'll* tell you what it's about—
ALICE. —point that finger at me again and it comes off—

(Lights up full.)

CHARLEY. It's about this brother and sister dance team from Manitoba—
MRS. STRAUS. *(To her husband.)* Not terribly original.
STRAUS. *(Indicating CHARLEY.)* Consider the source.
CHARLEY. He wants to be a hoofer, except she's gone and joined the American Political Woman's Union—
STRAUS. In Canada?
CHARLEY. *(To STRAUS.)* That's what *I* said. But don't worry. There's a happy ending after all. *(Glaring at ALICE.)* Because he saves her in the nick of time—just before they have her smoking cigars and shaving—
ALICE. When did you ever see me smoke a cigar?
CHARLEY. Well, you might as well! What's next, Alice?

Wrestling matches? Building railroads? Shootouts?
ALICE. If you think I'd audition anywhere with a pig-headed Nineteenth-Century clod like you—
CHARLEY. Then don't!

(ALICE stops dead.)

ALICE. What?
CHARLEY. I've already made emergency plans. *(Pause.)* It's okay, Alice. If you don't want to do it, I understand.
ALICE. Charley, you've never sung without me before! You couldn't carry a melody line by yourself if you got three laborers to lift it for you first.
CHARLEY. Oh, no? We'll just see about that. *(He sits at the piano and plays an opening riff. Singing.)* "Out west I have found, That's where hayseeds abound, And Missouri's the state that designed 'em. And though this may be you can take it from me, You don't have to go out west to find 'em. If you want to find the real hick delegation, The place where the real reubens dwell, Just hop on a train at the Grand Central Station, Get off when they shout 'New Rochelle!'"

(He plays a long lead-in. ALICE crosses her arms.)

ALICE. I'm waiting.

(Downstage, MRS. STRAUS looks up from her cards.)

MRS. STRAUS. *(Singing.)* "Only forty-five minutes from Broadway, Think of the changes it brings."
STRAUS. Ida! Wait! Come back!

(She rises and crosses up to CHARLEY.)

MRS. STRAUS. "For the short time it takes, What a difference it makes, In the way of the people and things."
CHARLEY. "Oh, what a swell bunch of reubens—"

MRS. STRAUS. "Oh, what a jay atmosphere—"
CHARLEY. "They have whiskers like hay—"
MRS. STRAUS. "And imagine Broadway—"
CHARLEY and MRS. STRAUS. "Only forty-five minutes from here."

(MRS. STRAUS turns to ALICE.)

MRS. STRAUS. Don't press your luck, dear.
ALICE. Charley, if this is your idea of a gag—
CHARLEY. Gee, that was jake, Mrs. S. You wanna try the soft shoe?
STRAUS. *(Rising.)* She most certainly does not!
MRS. STRAUS. Isidor, sit! *(To CHARLEY.)* Charley, dear, I've been thinking, and though I appreciate the offer, I believe the dance would work far better as a solo.
CHARLEY. Aw, come on, Mrs. S. You can't drop out now.

(A pause.)

MRS. STRAUS. That's not what I had in mind.
STRAUS. Oh, my God.
CHARLEY. *(To MRS. STRAUS.)* Well, if you think you can handle it—
ALICE. Charley, she's an old woman!
MRS. STRAUS. Choose those next words carefully, dear.
STRAUS. Ida, do be reasonable. Suppose someone should come in? Can you imagine what they'd say?

(Suddenly the downstage door is flung open, and ASTOR re-enters hurriedly, holding onto a slip of paper.)

ASTOR. Fortune, let me see that Marconigram from Cohan.
CHARLEY. Well, okay, but—I think they're casting younger. No offense.
ASTOR. *(To CHARLEY.)* Oh, don't be an idiot.
STRAUS. Has the whole *world* gone mad?

(He grabs the telegram from CHARLEY and crosses to the down center table, comparing the two slips of paper and deciphering as he does.)

ASTOR. Yes, it's as I thought. They're using those damned new international signals. How anyone is expected to eavesdrop successfully is quite beyond me.
MRS. STRAUS. How decidedly lower class. *(Eager.)* Eavesdrop on whom?
ASTOR. Young Phillips. Wireless operator. They're burning the air between here and Cape Race. Quite confidential, it seems.
ALICE. Then why did he let you in the cabin?
ASTOR. He's evidently been laboring under the delusion that I'm a personage of some rank with the steamship line. *(Frowning.)* Perhaps it's the way I dress.
STRAUS. Impressive, isn't it? The chain of command aboard this boat? The way one hand doesn't know who the other is, much less what he's doing, I'm surprised we haven't docked in Geneva.
CHARLEY. Switzerland is landlocked.
STRAUS. I'm aware of that.

(ASTOR looks up from his decoding.)

ASTOR. Well, here it is. As near as I can make out, we're taking in water at the bow.
CHARLEY. Are we *supposed* to be doin' that?
STRAUS. *(Mimicking.)* "No, we're not supposed to be doing that."
ALICE. He was only asking a question, Mr. Straus. *(To ASTOR.)* Captain Astor—
ASTOR. "Colonel."
ALICE. Is it serious?
ASTOR. Serious enough to be wiring other vessels, I'm afraid. Oh, don't be alarmed—we're in no danger. This is the Titanic, for God's sake.
STRAUS. Of course you would know. You were doubtless given three just like her for your eleventh birthday.

ALICE. What about the lifeboats?

CHARLEY. What lifeboats?

ALICE. Those white things hanging from the davits out there.

CHARLEY. Those are lifeboats?

ALICE. Of course they're lifeboats. What did you *think* they were?

CHARLEY. I thought they were planters.

MRS. STRAUS. Pardon me, but what does one *wear* in a lifeboat?

ASTOR. Please! All of you! Now, there doesn't appear to be any genuine distress. I'm convinced of it. After all, I didn't hear him sending out a "C.Q.D."

ALICE. I thought they stopped using that.

ASTOR. Even so. In the event of a real emergency, Im sure they'd revert to the more familiar signals.

(MRS. STRAUS peers over his shoulder and points to the paper.)

MRS. STRAUS. What does "S.O.S." mean?

ASTOR. Frankly, I haven't a clue.

STRAUS. Preposterous, Astor! If we're in no distress, why the devil are they sending for help?

ASTOR. Don't be primitive, Straus. To tow the ship to Halifax, obviously. It's the nearest port.

STRAUS. With a rip in her side?

ASTOR. What of it? The Titanic cannot go under!

STRAUS. I wish you'd all stop saying that! Don't you people read? The Titans—a mythical race of giants who ruled the earth for centuries. They didn't believe that anything could pierce them, either. Unfortunately, someone forgot to mention as much to Zeus.

CHARLEY. What happened?

STRAUS. You don't want to know. But I'd be most happy to tell you when—and if—we are ever privileged enough to behold the Brooklyn Bridge again.

MRS. STRAUS. Isidor—

STRAUS. Forgive me. I just wish I knew what nincompoop *named* this boat.

(The downstage door opens, and BRUCE ISMAY enters hesitantly. He stops short when he sees the group staring at him expectantly, then closes the door gently behind him, leans against it, and attempts to appear affable and unconcerned. There is a moment of silence; then, realizing that he's obviously going to have to say something, he speaks.)

ISMAY. Uh—guess what?

ASTOR. Bruce, for God's sake—

ISMAY. Now, it isn't as bad as it looks! A little hole, that's all! Why, it's barely three hundred feet long! And any feeble-minded fool knows the Titanic can float with every one of her first four compartments completely flooded. All right?

ASTOR. Just as a point of idle curiosity, Bruce—exactly how many of them *are* completely flooded?

ISMAY. No more than five! I swear it on my life!

STRAUS. Mr. Ismay, at present, that's not a very bankable guarantee.

ISMAY. It's quite the best I can do on short notice. Now, listen to me—

STRAUS. *(To MRS. STRAUS.)* Here comes the advertisement.

ISMAY. She's entirely able to remain above water indefinitely. Days, perhaps.

ASTOR. Really, Bruce. Wasn't she supposed to be indestructible?

ISMAY. *(Hesitating.)* More or less. So go to bed. Every one of you. As long as her bulkheads hold, there's no cause for alarm. Besides, the Carpathia is only 58 miles away, and—

ALICE. The Carpathia? If there's no cause for alarm, why did you call *them*?

ISMAY. I didn't! She just happens to be steaming in this direction.

ASTOR. "Happens to be"? In the middle of the night with no moon through an ice field? What's her destination, Bruce—Hell?

ALICE. Just a minute. *(Crossing to ISMAY.)* You don't mean to imply that we're sinking, do you?

ASTOR. Inconceivable.

ISMAY. Even if that were true, Miss, which I assure you it is not, a forty-six thousand ton steamship that cost ten million dollars and took three years to build does not sink. It founders.
MRS. STRAUS. Not with *me* on it, it doesn't.
STRAUS. Why? Who do *you* know?

(MRS. STRAUS takes ISMAY's arm and pulls him aside, as ASTOR crosses to the portholes and begins peering outside anxiously.)

MRS. STRAUS. Mr. Ismay. Dear. I have this nasty little niece who plays the flute quite badly, and she's giving a recital next Friday evening at 8:00 sharp. It's the only way she can get anyone to listen to her. Generally, we manage to be ill, but if we miss it again this year and she finds out it's because our ship has sunk, she's liable to think we did it on purpose. Now, I'm sure you could find some way of fixing that leak, couldn't you? Perhaps if you were to stuff it with torn bedding or unwashed table linens or third-class baggage? We'll pay for any incidental expenses, of course.
ISMAY. That won't be necessary. Thomas Andrews is on board. Of Harland and Wolff? And I feel quite confident that he's doing whatever can be done.
ASTOR. Who the devil is Thomas Andrews?
ISMAY. The man who built this ship.
CHARLEY. Oh, swell.
STRAUS. Listen to the young man, Ismay. Swell, indeed.
ISMAY. Mr. Straus, the day I am wretched enough to solicit advice from an actor, you shall find me instead retiring to Wales with a pint of brandy and a sheepdog!
ASTOR. Good God! Kitty! She must be beside herself!
MRS. STRAUS. How fortunate that she has that option. And your wife. Whom is *she* beside?
ASTOR. I beg your pardon?
MRS. STRAUS. Madeleine. *(Pause.) You* know—that striking brunette with the opal earrings and the barest trace of a smile. Surely, you've seen her aboard. If not, I shall point her out to you—
ALICE. *(To ISMAY.)* Don't ever talk to my brother that way again—

ISMAY. Really, Miss Cohan—

(ASTOR turns to STRAUS, puzzled.)

ASTOR. *(Indicating ALICE.)* Miss who?
STRAUS. It's not worth the explanation.
ISMAY. *(To ALICE.)* I see no need for hostility—
ALICE. Forgive me. I've been inclined toward bad manners ever since I discovered "drowning" on today's schedule of activities.
ISMAY. Please, Miss. Now that the Carpathia is on her way, there's a very simple solution to all of this—
CHARLEY. Yeah. "Sail Cunard."
ISMAY. *(To CHARLEY.)* Mr. Cohan, were I you, I'd hardly feel entitled to throw stones at the mistakes of others. *(Pause.)* I saw *Popularity*—and my only criticism was that you chose to call it a play. "Bilge" would not have been an inappropriate term.

(CHARLEY's mouth drops open.)

CHARLEY. I- I- I- I-

(He turns to ALICE, frantically telegraphing for help. There's a pause.)

ALICE. Go on. Let's see you get out of *this* one.

(CHARLEY turns back to ISMAY.)

CHARLEY. H-H-H-How—how can you say that?!
ISMAY. Having been forced to sit through it, I've purchased the right to say whatever I damned well please—
CHARLEY. I- I- I- I-

(ALICE pushes him aside.)

ALICE. That's enough, George. *(To ISMAY.)* Mr. Ismay, perhaps it's true that *Popularity* was not up to my brother's usually impeccable standards. He has, after all, had two theatres, four

boulevards and a trolley depot named after him—
 CHARLEY. *(Under his breath.)* I have?

(She kicks him.)

ALICE. So I need not tire you with his credentials. But in his defense, I should point out that when my brother strikes an iceberg, at least he's back in six months with a new show. *Broadway Jones*? You may have heard of it. We go into rehearsal in September. Why, just ask the Colossus of Rothes—
 CHARLEY. *(Hissing.)* "Countess." OW!
 ALICE. Tell me, Mr. Ismay. What does White Star have planned for the fall? A chance encounter with a glacier?
 ISMAY. Miss Cohan—
 ALICE. If not, I'm sure you can find a convenient barrier reef somewhere between Southampton and—
 ISMAY. Really, I don't think you're being altogether fair—
 ALICE. Fair?! Oh, heavens, is that the object of this voyage? Then surely you won't mind a simple question. WHAT IF THE CARPATHIA DOESN'T GET HERE IN TIME?!?

(ASTOR turns around suddenly.)

ASTOR. She already has.

(The others look up.)

STRAUS. What?

(ASTOR points out of the porthole.)

ASTOR. Look for yourself.
ISMAY. Wait—

(With the exception of ISMAY, they all rush to the windows.)

STRAUS. I don't see anything.

ISMAY. That's because—
ASTOR. Right over there. About five miles off the stern. If that isn't a Royal Mail Steamer, then I'm a Vanderbilt.
ISMAY. I wouldn't—
ALICE. Thank God!
MRS. STRAUS. Oh, Isidor—
CHARLEY. *(To ALICE.)* A trolley depot?!?
ALICE. Don't be a snob.
STRAUS. Astor, are you sure that's the Carpathia?
ISMAY. No—
ASTOR. For God's sake, Straus, what do you *think* it is—a sea urchin with a starboard lamp? Of course it's the Carpathia. Who else could it be?
ISMAY. Uh—we think she's a freighter.
ASTOR. Really, Bruce. What difference does pedigree make at a time like this? She's here, isn't she?
ISMAY. In a sense—

(ALICE turns to CHARLEY.)

ALICE. I'm sorry if I called you a Nineteenth-Century clod.
CHARLEY. Sorry enough to do the song with me?
ALICE. No.
CHARLEY. *(Calling out.)* Mrs. S!
ALICE. All right, you little twit!
CHARLEY. Hot dog!

(He grabs her arm and begins pulling her toward the piano, as MRS. STRAUS turns to her husband and indicates the distant ship.)

MRS. STRAUS. And you were alarmed.
STRAUS. I wouldn't take me to court yet. Like a cabbage soup, it still smells.

(CHARLEY plops ALICE down on the piano bench and plays a lead-in.)

ALICE. Oh, Charley—now?
CHARLEY. Come on. We've only got a week to get great.
ISMAY. Please! All of you—
CHARLEY. *(Singing.)* "Push me along in my pushcart, Push me along with the crowd, What a sensational feeling one feels, It beats all the airships and automobiles."
ALICE. *(Singing.)* "Covered with carrots and rhubarb, Over the sidewalks we shout, Oh, what adventures a single girl meets—"
CHARLEY. "—peddling vegetables out in the streets—"
ALICE. "Did you ever get kissed through a wet bunch of beets?"
CHARLEY and ALICE. "When you're pushed along in your pushcart—"

(ASTOR turns around suddenly, in time to catch ISMAY sneaking out the door.)

ASTOR. Just a moment!

(They all freeze. ISMAY straightens up.)

ASTOR. Bruce, much as I dislike casting doubt upon an obvious gift from the Almighty, that ship doesn't seem to be drawing any closer.
STRAUS. *(To his wife.)* You see?
ISMAY. Yes, well, there's a reason for that.
ALICE. Then perhaps we'd better hear it.

(CHARLEY turns to her.)

CHARLEY. Says who?
ISMAY. You understand of course that this is not yet official—
ASTOR. It never is.
ISMAY. —but it appears as if they've all gone to sleep.
CHARLEY. THEY'VE WHAT?!
ISMAY. Don't worry—we're attempting to rouse them now. If our signals dont work, we'll try rockets. They've got to wake up

sooner or later.

STRAUS. Have you contemplated torpedoes?

ISMAY. If you don't mind, Straus—

ASTOR. Of course he minds, Ismay! Wouldn't you? I should think that the imbecilic flair with which this boat seems to attract catastrophe is grounds enough for—

ISMAY. DAMMIT! DO YOU SUPPOSE I PLANNED IT THIS WAY? FIRST I FIND A FRAYED DRAPE IN THE DINING SALOON AND NOW THIS! I DETEST SUNDAYS!

ASTOR. Now, see here, Bruce—

ISMAY. Oh, don't condescend to me, you obsequious ass. I'd prefer a hundred obdurate stonemasons to one ingrate such as yourself!

ASTOR. Ingrate?!

ISMAY. Ingrate indeed! *(Indicating the ship.)* Whom exactly do you think all of this was for? Me? Precisely whose excesses do you presume the Titanic was commissioned to indulge? Mine? Do you seriously believe that I conceived the epigenesis of the largest moving object in the world solely because it made me feel important?

ALL. Yes.

ISMAY. What of it! It's about time somebody put an end to this ridiculous practice of colloquy between the classes. I find it demeaning enough that we must share the hearth with them in the first place—I see no need for practicing tolerance on the high seas as well.

STRAUS. Rubbish. You carry steerage on board the same as everyone else.

ISMAY. Yes—but barricaded below and used primarily for weight distribution. And in the event of a punctured hull, we needn't worry about a costly alarm system, for when enough of them have drowned, we know it's time to wire for help.

(The door opens. MURDOCH enters.)

MURDOCH. Mr. Ismay, they're preparing to send off—
ISMAY. *(Indicating MURDOCH.)* Case in point. Murdoch.
MURDOCH. Sir.

ISMAY. What is the correct room temperature of an 1888 Chateau Larose served with filet de boeuf?
MURDOCH. Fifty-eight degrees, sir. Provided it's been allowed to breathe for—
ISMAY. Murdoch!
MURDOCH. *(By rote.)* I don't know, sir.
ISMAY. And how does one properly address a belted earl?
MURDOCH. I'm sure I don't know, sir.
ISMAY. Excellent. Tell me—who wrote *La Gioconda*?
MURDOCH. Gilbert and Sullivan, sir. Will that be all?
ISMAY. Murdoch?
MURDOCH. Sir?
ISMAY. Get out.
MURDOCH. Indeed, sir.

(He exits. ISMAY turns to the others.)

ISMAY. Three ships, Colonel Astor. The Olympic, the Gigantic, and the Titanic. *(Indicating MURDOCH's exit.)* Each designed as a sanctuary from *that,* and one of them—one in particular—calculated to make God blush for not having thought of her first.
MRS. STRAUS. Come now, Mr. Ismay. Don't be modest.
ISMAY. Madam, I can assure you that modesty is the only perquisite this vessel does not own. I doubt that the Garden of Eden contained a jeweled copy of Khayyam's *Rubaiyat*, don't you? I find it just as unlikely that the walls of Jericho were forged with double-plated steel. And to my knowledge, the Bible doesn't once mention hand-cut crystal or stained glass when speaking of the Promised Land. The Philistines never could have paid the price.
STRAUS. I don't believe—
ISMAY. Then you're a fool! The Titanic has been inscribed with every successive conquest of man's intellect, and dammit, I should know! I saw to it myself!

(From outside, we hear a muffled explosion.)

ISMAY. Good God!

(He races out the door; CHARLEY turns to ALICE.)

CHARLEY. How can they do this to us? We have an audition!

ALICE. *(Mimicking ISMAY's accent.)* "Oh, don't be alarmed. Thomas Andrews is on board. He's the man who *built* this ship."

STRAUS. Thomas Andrews, indeed. Leave it to Ismay to pour oil on the flame.

MRS. STRAUS. What on earth am I going to tell my niece? She's chosen *Claire de Lune*. In E-flat. No doubt the others will be playing in B.

(CHARLEY turns to ALICE.)

CHARLEY. Sis, I'm gonna wake up Father. Mother and the girls ought to be ready in case—

ALICE. In case what? Charley, this isn't a dime novel hidden in the corncrib. I'm sure it's just—

(CHARLEY yanks open the downstage right door. From outside, we hear the rumble of several hundred passengers surging onto the boat deck. CHARLEY points.)

CHARLEY. What, Alice? A convention? Come on. I'm not gonna lose you, too.

(He grabs her arm and drags her out the door. Moments later, we hear MURDOCH's voice—)

MURDOCH *(O.S.)*. Stand back! All of you! First class only!

(—and a gunshot. In seconds, CHARLEY and ALICE are back inside, slamming the door shut behind them and looking at one another, white-faced.)

CHARLEY. All right. We'll wait 'til the Carpathia gets here, and then—

ALICE. Charley, we won't have to. I mean, any minute now

they'll turn on the engines, and—

(*From off to the side, ASTOR turns around suddenly.*)

    ASTOR. How does it go, exactly?
    STRAUS. How does *what* go?
    ASTOR. *(Reciting.)* "For I dipped into the future, Far as human eye could see, Saw the Vision of the world, And all the wonders that would be. Saw the heavens fill with commerce, Argosies of magic sails, Pilots of the purple twilight, Dropping down with costly bales."
    STRAUS. Intriguing you should choose Tennyson at a time like this. I'd have quoted Poe.
    ASTOR. I can't quite remember the way it ends.
    STRAUS. You can indeed. Perhaps it's simply that you'd rather not.

(*Suddenly, they all reach out for support as the chandelier begins to sway. ASTOR, paling, regains his balance and stares front.*)

    ASTOR. "Not in vain the distance beacons, Forward, forward, let us range. Let the people spin forever, Down the ringing grooves of change."

(*Instinctively, all but ASTOR stare down toward the ocean through the smoking room floor, then look back up at one another slowly.*)

ACT I CURTAIN

ACT II

(At curtain rise, we see STRAUS, MRS. STRAUS, and ALICE clustered around the stage left portholes, peering out into the night. ASTOR, his pipe lit, is seated at the down left table, facing front and appearing unconcerned.)

ALICE. Can you see my brother?
MRS. STRAUS. Alice, dear—I'm sure there's no reason to be concerned.
STRAUS. Don't indulge her, Ida. She knows better than that.

(ASTOR chuckles to himself as the door opens; CHARLEY races into the room, tearing toward one of the portholes.)

ALICE. Charley, where are they?
CHARLEY. I don't know. They weren't in the cabin, and Mother's coat was gone. *(Pointing outside.)* They've got to be out there someplace. *(Turning to STRAUS.)* Has the freighter spotted us yet?
STRAUS. It wouldn't appear so.
CHARLEY. *(Calling outside.)* Wake up, you pathetic fools!
MRS. STRAUS. Shouldn't we attempt to signal them?
ALICE. Yes! I saw a lantern on the promenade.
CHARLEY. Swell. Where's the kerosene?
STRAUS. The British probably drank it.
CHARLEY. Then we— *(Looking closer.)* Wait! It's moving!

(As they all lean in to stare, the upstage door opens and two figures enter stealthily. One of them is a reluctant THOMAS KILGANNON, who is now attired in an ill-fitting tuxedo about

two sizes too small that looks as though he's swiped it from one of the swells in first class (which come to think of it is probably what he did); the other is MARY CANAVAN, a young, pretty, and poorly dressed Irish immigrant, who is prying her arm loose from THOMAS' grip, which is perhaps less protective than amorous. Pointing urgently toward the downstage door, she pushes him across the room; as they reach the bar, he stops, spies a bottle of brandy, and grabs it—pantomiming to MARY how cold it is outside. Shaking it once, however, he realizes it is practically empty, and so indicates that she exit to the boat deck ahead of him, as he ducks behind the bar in search of a full bottle. MARY impatiently heads toward the down right door.)

ALICE. I don't think so, Charley.
CHARLEY. Yeah, it is. Can't you see?
ALICE. Where are you looking?
CHARLEY. Over there. At the blinking light.
ALICE. That isn't a freighter. It's Venus.
STRAUS. This is ridiculous. I'm sure they'd spot the lantern. (To *ALICE*.) On the promenade, did you say?
ALICE. *(Pointing.)* Yes. Just beyond—

(They all turn in time to see MARY at the door. There is a pause.)

CHARLEY. Uh—hello?

(MARY pivots, frantic.)

MARY. The gate was open. Nobody stopped me! I got me immigration papers! I know me rights! Come any closer and I'll scream!

(A pause. STRAUS turns to his wife.)

STRAUS. You had to go to Europe, didn't you? Atlantic City wasn't good enough.
MARY. *(To ASTOR.)* Please, sir. If you've even a shred of

Catholic charity, you won't report me. *(Pointing.)* I've got to get out there and find me—me Mum! She's lookin' for a—for a new leg—
CHARLEY. On the boat deck?
MARY. In New York! They're all out in Lahardane. And if we don't be arrivin' on time, she may die.
ASTOR. *(Rising.)* Of course I won't report you. What do you take me for?
MARY. I'd rather not say, sir.

(MRS. STRAUS turns to her husband.)

MRS. STRAUS. Look at the poor thing, Isidor. Surely someone can assist her.
CHARLEY. Yeah. If the old lady's really gonna pipe off—
STRAUS. Young man, assuming you are permitted access to the rest of your life, which at the moment represents an imposition on logic, I wouldn't recommend a career in diplomacy. *(Mumbling.)* "Pipe off"....

(ALICE crosses to MARY.)

ALICE. Won't you sit down, Miss—
MARY. Canavan, if it's all the same. And no, I don't believe I will. It wouldn't be proper. Not here.
ALICE. Please. Social amenities mean nothing at a time like this.
ASTOR. I beg your pardon, but on East Sixty-Fifth Street they do. We strive to avoid exception.
ALICE. Major?
ASTOR. "Colonel."
ALICE. Shut up. *(To MARY.)* Now, why don't you make yourself comfortable while I look for—
MARY. Thankin' you, Miss, but if you'll just be pointin' me to the boat deck—
ALICE. It's—it's out that way. But wouldn't you like to bring your mother inside and have her lie down for a few minutes? There's really no need to hurry.

MARY. Oh, she'll be fine once we've got away from these Halls of Hell—

(From behind the bar, we hear a sneeze.)

MARY. God bless.
THOMAS' VOICE. Thank you.

(MARY winces, then opens the door.)

MARY. Divil a bit of a cold meself. Water everywhere—and me in me stockin' feet. Well, I'll just be goin'. Ever so sorry to have troubled you fine people.
ASTOR. One moment.

(He crosses behind the bar and pulls THOMAS up by the hair.)

THOMAS. OW! Watch what ye'll be doin', mate.

(He straightens out his tie, adjusts his jacket, then extends a hand.)

THOMAS. Kilgannon's the name. We'd just be— *(Looking closer.)* Oh, it's you, is it? I—
ASTOR. As I thought. *(To MARY.)* A new leg?

(They all glare at her. Stumped, she turns back to THOMAS and fakes it.)

MARY. What have you done with me Mum?
THOMAS. Didn't I be tippin' the wink all right? There'll be daylights to pay for not comin' up the back stairs.
MARY. And who told you to go and sneeze, you ill-mannered hell-hound?
THOMAS. Whad'ye want me to do now—hold it in and be blowin' me ears out?
ALICE. *(To MARY.)* Do you know this man?
MARY. I never set eyes on him before in me life.

THOMAS. Not eyes, p'raps—
MARY. That was an accident.
THOMAS. And how would it be an accident, Mary? Yer mouth just happened to be bumpin' into mine?
CHARLEY. *(To THOMAS.)* Now, look here, fella—
ASTOR. I'll handle this.

(He grabs THOMAS by the front.)

ASTOR. You call yourself a male, you unspeakable blight on the gender? You dare to rank yourself with the brave generals and captains and heroes of war whose birthright you share? What have you got to say for yourself?
THOMAS. *(Indicating his suspenders.)* Ye'll be getting' yer hands off the braces then. They cost *somebody* dear.
STRAUS. Good God! Has the boy no shame at all?
THOMAS. Afraid not, old salt. Sold it to pay for me passage on this biscuit tin. *(To MARY.)* When was I bein' ill-mannered?
MARY. Don't you touch me, you—you human spittoon! *(To the others.)* He means nothin' to me! I swear! I said to him, "Theodore," I said—
THOMAS. It's Thomas.
MARY. You told me it was Theodore!
THOMAS. And when would I be tellin' ye that?
MARY. Down below! On the stairway!
THOMAS. It was dark on the stairway. Likely ye wouldn't be hearin' it proper.
MARY. Indeed I would. I was holdin' onto the railing when—
THOMAS. Ye'd be holdin' onto me hand—
MARY. And I promise you I wasn't enjoyin' the experience.
THOMAS. Ye wouldn't be givin' me half a chance now either. I— *(To CHARLEY.)* What'll *ye* be starin' at?
CHARLEY. You're in tails.
THOMAS. And what're *ye* supposed to be, mate? A parade?
ASTOR. Didn't I see Mr. Guggenheim wearing that coat last evening?
THOMAS. And what if he was? They give me a berth right next

to the luggage hold, don't ye know. When the water started, a suitcase floated into me room. I thought they'd be wantin' me to *have* it now. Get out of me way—

MRS. STRAUS. Mr. Kilgannon, there must be some mistake. Why, as long as the bulkheads hold, there *is* no water.

STRAUS. Listen to you. Captain Ahab.

THOMAS. Oh, there'll be no water, will there? Then why would me and Martin be comin' up here twice already, tell me that?

ALICE. Martin who?

THOMAS. Gallagher. Me best friend. He got Ellie Mockler onto a boat and seven others besides. I done the same for Margareth Mannion. Give her me jumper too, I did. It's cold out there. *(To ASTOR.)* So go on. Be tellin' me I've no title to a shirt for me efforts, and I'll be pushin' yer eyes out through the back of yer head.

ASTOR. I think you'd best be going. This facility was not designed for roughnecks.

THOMAS. Ye'll be startin' to get on me nerves bye and bye. Haven't ye got tables to wait?

ASTOR. Do you know who I *am*?

THOMAS. And do I care?

ASTOR. If that's the way you'd like it played, I'll have you *thrown* out.

MRS. STRAUS. Oh, Colonel, don't. He's positively touching.

STRAUS. He is? I suppose that's the type of son-in-law you'd prefer.

MRS. STRAUS. Why not? We could take him to one of Mrs. Rothschild's tiresome garden parties.

STRAUS. And never be invited back again.

MRS. STRAUS. Yes. *(To THOMAS.)* Do you play pinochle, Mr. Kilgannon?

THOMAS. Sorry, Bridey. The only one I'd be knowin' is Ballinamore Bridge.

MRS. STRAUS. I'm not familiar with it.

THOMAS. Well, it'll be yer basic five-card stud, 'ceptin' him who'd be losin' pulls off all his clothes. How about a round?

STRAUS. Certainly not!

THOMAS. And why not indeed, old salt? Can't ye be takin' the competition?

STRAUS. Young man, it isn't the competition I object to—it's the aroma.

THOMAS. Then have it like ye will. Only I'll not be leavin' here without me girl.

MARY. Your what?!

THOMAS. Oh, Mary—me brother John in the Bronx'll put up two the same as one. I'd even be sleepin' on the floor if ye'd have it so.

MARY. You would, would you? And do you take me for one of Mrs. Warren's women you can flatter with an indecent proposal?

THOMAS. I'm a Galway man. It's the only kind we'd be knowin' how to make now.

CHARLEY. *(To ALICE.)* Who's Mrs. Warren?

ALICE. Another pioneer, Charles.

MARY. *(To THOMAS.)* Mr. Kilgannon, if you fancy I came all this way to take up with a total stranger and a Jack Nasty to boot—

THOMAS. What stranger? It'll be fourteen minutes on the bye.

MARY. Thirteen and a half. And I've hated every one of them. Besides, what would we be tellin' our children, assumin' we were so blessed, when they asked us where we met? On the second step from the bottom?

THOMAS. Mary, don't ye believe in God?

MARY. Wash out your mouth, you foul-tempered good-for-naught! I wouldn't be teachin' church school if I was a heathen such as yourself now, would I? And what's He got to do with it anyway?

THOMAS. Only everything! I'd have been on the Oceanic but for there not bein' enough coal to go around. D'ye really think I'd be havin' the idea to sail this bucket of bolts on me own? Martin, now, he's fit to be tied. "Titanic," says he when he caught her size. "Over me dead body." Evidently, they'll be agreein' with him! Coal strike, indeed. But for the Almighty, how *else* d'ye suppose I'd be turnin' up here?

MRS. STRAUS. It certainly wasn't the luck of the Irish.

THOMAS. Oh, Mary—don't ye see? The Good Lord wanted us to meet. He meant for it to happen.

(A thoughtful pause.)

MARY. Go on with ye. He meant nothin' of the kind.

(CHARLEY taps THOMAS on the shoulder.)

CHARLEY. Good try, though.
THOMAS. I love you—
MARY. Go away—
THOMAS. Take me blood—
MARY. And what would I do with it, tell me that—
THOMAS. Mary, there's nothin' ye'll be sayin' to change me mind.
MARY. Oh, Thomas—I'm engaged!
STRAUS. *(To his wife.)* That should be sufficient.
THOMAS. Y'are not.
MARY. I am indeed. To a hatmaker in San Francisco. And he'd be havin' the fits if he could see you now.
THOMAS. A hatmaker?
MARY. And what if he is? He loves me fierce. Or me picture anyway.
THOMAS. But he makes hats.
MARY. Yes. *(Pause.)* Men's hats.
THOMAS. And what'll he be doin' for a livin' then?
MARY. Here, I'll not have you speakin' of me betrothed in such a fashion.
THOMAS. And I'll not be botherin'. Just tell me his name that I might be rippin' his throat out.
MARY. It's— it's— *(She reaches into her pocket and pulls out a slip of paper. Squinting at it for a moment, she turns to ALICE.)* Miss?

(ALICE crosses to her and stares down at the handwriting.)

MARY. Does that say "Stuart" or "Steven"?
ALICE. "Scott".
MARY. Oh. *(Reading.)* "Scott MacKay, 12 Geary Street." *(To THOMAS.)* He's me brother Pat's best friend. So there. You can believe it or don't—'tis all the same to me, for I never want to see you again!

(She crosses to the downstage door.)

THOMAS. Mary, wait! Please!

(CHARLEY leaps for the piano and begins to play.)

CHARLEY. *(Singing.)* "So long Mary, Mary we will miss you so. So long Mary, How we hate to see you go—" *(MARY freezes, her hand on the knob.)* "And we'll all be longing for you Mary, While you roam. So long Mary, Don't forget to come back home."

(She pulls open the door and slams it shut behind her as she exits. There's a pause. Then THOMAS turns to CHARLEY.)

THOMAS. That'll be one I owe ye, mate.
CHARLEY. Why? It didn't work.

(The door opens and MARY re-enters. She crosses up to THOMAS.)

MARY. I only come back because of the music.
THOMAS. I can be tellin' that.
MARY. And bein' away from you, however briefly, did nothin' to change me feelings.
THOMAS. Indeed.
MARY. So I trust you'll be keepin' your distance?
THOMAS. I won't be puttin' a hand to you. I swear.
MARY. As long as I have your word. *(There is a sudden explosion from outside and a white glare reflecting in from the portholes. MARY is instantly in Kilgannon's arms.)* Oh, Thomas!
ASTOR. What the devil was that?

(He and the others race stage left and stare outside, leaving MARY and THOMAS locked in an embrace center stage. There is another explosion.)

STRAUS. Distress rockets.
ASTOR. It's about damned well time.

CHARLEY. Golly, aren't they setting them off kinda close?

ALICE. *(Sarcastic.)* You're right, Charley. If they're not careful, they might damage the ship.

MRS. STRAUS. You don't suppose we could sail the *iceberg* back to New York, do you?

(As they all lean in closer, MARY pulls away from Tom's arms.)

MARY. Oh, Thomas—this is all me own fault.

THOMAS. And why'd ye be sayin' a thing like that?

MARY. You won't hate me?

THOMAS. Could I?

MARY. Me Mum read me cups and told me a storm'd be gatherin' about me head if I didn't listen to me brother Pat.

THOMAS. Who'd be tellin' ye what?

MARY. "ary, wait a year. I'll bring you over then." Sure it wasn't me doin' that Johnny Bourke's cousin made all that money in Chicago and sent for half of Lahardane now. Thomas, if I'd stayed the year, I'd have had nobody to go to Confession with.

THOMAS. And what'll ye be confessin'?

MARY. Nothin', I'm sure.

THOMAS. I could change that.

MARY. Indeed. And what about Margareth Mannion? I couldn't be missin' the smile in your eye when you'd speak her name now, could I?

THOMAS. Ye'd be readin' passion for a dustball. Me word on it.

MARY. I'm a married woman.

THOMAS. *(Reaching for her.)* Not yet.

MARY. I'll be thankin' you to remember before touchin' me again that I teach the Good Book to very young children.

THOMAS. *(Moving closer.)* I'm very young children then. Teach me.

(A pause.)

MARY. Blow your nose. You look like Lucifer himself.

THOMAS. Have you got a 'kerchief, Mary? Guggenheim's were wet.

(She reaches into her skirt pocket and pulls out a handkerchief. As she touches it to his cheek, their eyes lock. In moments, their faces begin drawing closer and closer.)

ALICE. What are they waiting for?
MRS. STRAUS. The suspense is dreadful.
CHARLEY. Boy, you think they'd have made a move by now.
STRAUS. Perhaps she's just being careful.
ASTOR. Do you blame her? She doesn't want to get rammed.
THOMAS. *(Raises his head, startled.)* What?

(THOMAS and MARY consummate the kiss.)

MRS. STRAUS. Certainly they'll see it. Why, at any moment, they're bound to—I mean, I'm sure they'll—

(They all lean in closer. Another explosion, followed by a beat.)

CHARLEY. WHAT DO THEY THINK IT IS—THE FOURTH OF JULY?!?

(THOMAS and MARY pull apart hastily. MARY sits down and withdraws a piece of knitting as the others move away from the portholes. STRAUS turns to his wife.)

STRAUS. Carpathia or not, my dear, I do believe it's time we said goodbye to this ship.
THOMAS. The old gent's got a point. Before she'll be sayin' goodbye to *us*.
ASTOR. I don't recall anyone soliciting *your* endorsement.
THOMAS. How'd ye take to kissin' me foot?
ASTOR. And how would you like a sound beating?
THOMAS. Comin' from the likes of you? A bib-and-tucker who'll be wearin' skinny breeches? Tell me, mate. When ye fart,

d'yer shoes blow off?
ASTOR. Really!

(A pause.)

MRS. STRAUS. Well, *do* they?
STRAUS. That's entirely enough. Ida, get your coat. You heard the young man. It's cold out there.
MRS. STRAUS. Oh, Isidor—a lifeboat? How indecorous. Isn't there some other way?
STRAUS. For God's sake, what would you like me to do—call a taxi?

(THOMAS crosses upstage right to the bar. His back to the others, he begins pouring himself a drink. ALICE turns to CHARLEY.)

ALICE. Charles, I'll look for Mother and the girls. You look for Father.
CHARLEY. Right. Where do I meet you?
ALICE. Back here. If—
STRAUS. Preposterous. That deck is crawling with people. You'll never make it through twice.
MRS. STRAUS. I'm afraid he's correct. Perhaps if one of you were to locate your family and board a different boat—
ALICE. That's out of the question.
MRS. STRAUS. Alice, dear—I'm sure they'll be quite safe.
ALICE. You don't understand.
MRS. STRAUS. Of course I do.
ALICE. I couldn't possibly—
STRAUS. Don't be foolish—
ALICE. —there must be another way—
ASTOR. —it appears you have no choice—
ALICE. I'M NOT LEAVING THIS SHIP WITHOUT MY BROTHER!
ASTOR. Then dammit, you'd better come up with an alternative!

CHARLEY. If you swear like that in front of her again, it'll be the last thing you do.

STRAUS. At the moment, Mr. Fortune, what *isn't*?

ASTOR. Oh, for God's sake! This is idiotic! The very notion that this vessel would concede to anything other than sailing proudly only proves what can happen to human logic when it's exposed repeatedly to the cinema. Mark my words—moving pictures will be the death of us all. Not icebergs.

MRS. STRAUS. Are you coming, Colonel?

ASTOR. Certainly not! *(Pointing to the boat deck.)* Mrs. Straus, have you ever attempted your way through a mob such as that?

MRS. STRAUS. No. *(Pause.)* But I've got a maid who has.

ASTOR. Precisely. And I have a manservant. Without them, we should be eaten alive. And for what? To return here the complete fool at daybreak? No, thank you.

STRAUS. Come now, Astor. You were a war hero, weren't you? Surely you must have charged a brigade or stormed a fortress or whatever it is they do these days.

ASTOR. If you must know, I designed batteries for the American army.

CHARLEY. Batteries?! And you got made an *officer* for that?!?

ASTOR. They were *very popular* batteries.

ALICE. Marvelous. Now we don't have to shove our way through that crowd. You can show us how to electrocute them instead.

ASTOR. I find your lack of respect appalling. *(To CHARLEY.)* And if you know what's best for yourself, you'll do just as I.

CHARLEY. Marry somebody half my age?

ASTOR. HAVE A DRINK AND RETIRE FOR THE NIGHT!

MRS. STRAUS. How does one "shove", exactly?

STRAUS. It's done with the arms.

MRS. STRAUS. Like this?

STRAUS. For God's sake, Ida—you look as though you've a broken hip!

ASTOR. What difference does it make? You don't stand a chance on your own. This requires an ill-bred ruffian who has neither manners nor—

(They all look up simultaneously. Slowly their heads turn upstage right. THOMAS is at the bar, facing the area behind it so that he can't see them. There is a pause. Then he speaks.)

THOMAS. So me stock'll be goin' up, will it?
STRAUS. Mr. Kilgannon—
THOMAS. Forget it, mate. Ye'd be hurtin' me feelings.
ALICE. He's going to pout. We're trapped and he's going to pout. I'll give him another thirty seconds and then—
CHARLEY. Alice, don't. He won't be any help at all if he's bleeding.
MRS. STRAUS. *(To THOMAS.)* Young man, I'm sure that whatever indelicate remarks you may have overheard were entirely accidental. *(A glare.) Weren't* they, Colonel Astor?

(THOMAS indicates the boat deck.)

THOMAS. And just why would ye be needin' *me* out there now?
ASTOR. Because you're a bilious—
MRS. STRAUS. What he means is that you're more accustomed to that sort of behavior than we are.
STRAUS. Doing what it is that you do, after all.
THOMAS. Which is what, would ye be sayin'?
CHARLEY. Laying bricks?
ALICE. Selling vegetables?
MRS. STRAUS. Sweeping chimneys? *(Hastily.)* The better ones, of course.

(A pause. THOMAS sighs.)

THOMAS. P'raps ye should be readin' Yeats instead of Dickens then. 'Tis a different little island, ye know. *(Pause.)* I'm an agricultural laborer.
MRS. STRAUS. What does that mean?
THOMAS. Me and Marty'd be shovellin' dung and cuttin' peat for Matt Kilcommons down by the old bog road. Sure ye wouldn't be tellin' me *that'll* gain me papers to the upper classes now, would ye?

ASTOR. Indeed not! *(Pointing.)* Those are people out there—not livestock.

THOMAS. I'd be lookin' again if I was you. We're *all* travellin' steerage now.

MRS. STRAUS. Please, Mr. Kilgannon—

THOMAS. All right—I'll be strikin' a bargain with you.

ASTOR. For the love of God—

THOMAS. No. For a job. Our night stay in Cork'd be seven and six on us apiece—and meself startin' out with twenty pounds and two cuff buttons! If I'm to be getting' ye from here to there—

STRAUS. I'll make you a stock boy.

THOMAS. Christmas off?

STRAUS. But you work Yom Kippur.

MRS. STRAUS. *(To Mr. STRAUS.)* I told you he could be trusted.

THOMAS. All right, then. *(Pointing to ASTOR.)* Only first, he'll be havin' to say he likes me.

ASTOR. What, me? Never!

STRAUS. Really, Astor. At a time like this—

ASTOR. At a time like what? I don't wish to live *that* badly. What would I have left? A hundred millions and no principles.

THOMAS. Ye'd be interested in a trade then?

ASTOR. I'd be interested in nothing of the kind!

THOMAS. Then I thank ye.

ASTOR. For what?

THOMAS. Me nephew Michael'd be askin' me to send him a photograph of a real American. If ye'd be what he had in mind, the likeness of his own backside'd be doin' the job just as well, and he wouldn't be needin' a picture of that now, would he?

ASTOR. See here. I have no intention of setting foot in one of those—those—dinghies! Because if I did—

THOMAS. —if ye did, ye'd be comin' face up to knowin' that everything ye ever believed in was a lie.

ASTOR. IF THIS SHIP CAN BE SUNK, DAMMIT, YOU MIGHT JUST AS WELL SCUTTLE THE ENTIRE HUMAN RACE! DO YOU PRESUME TO QUESTION A CHAMPION?

(THOMAS chuckles.)

THOMAS. Champion, indeed. 'Tis the Creator's little miracles ye people'd be overlookin', mate. Like the grass ye'd be walkin' on and the air ye'd breathe. And He wouldn't be usin' ice to send a champion to the bottom of the Atlantic now, would He? Only a Challenger.

(A pause. ASTOR is white-faced.)

ASTOR. That's ridiculous.
THOMAS. Prove it then.

(ASTOR looks around the room, pale and uncertain for the first time. After glancing at each of the others, he turns back to THOMAS and mumbles to himself.)

ASTOR. If the Board of Directors ever finds out I've taken orders from a dirt farmer, the entire empire is in danger of collapse.
THOMAS. Now ye'll be talkin'. *(To CHARLEY.)* Mate, ye ever be rowin' a boat before?
CHARLEY. Almost once, at Lake Tonawanda, when—
THOMAS. Well, ye don't know what ye've been missin'. You and me, we'll be takin' the right oar. *(To ASTOR.)* You. Waiter. Ye'll be takin' the left.
STRAUS. With me, I presume.
THOMAS. Ye'll be holdin' yer tongue.
STRAUS. Young man, are you implying that I'm not fit enough?
THOMAS. Look here—in Corrafarry where I come from, a gent who'll get to be as old as you has things done *for* him. So ring off.
STRAUS. Indeed. *(To MRS. STRAUS.)* Do we have any holdings in Corrafarry?
MRS. STRAUS. No.
STRAUS. Let's get some.
THOMAS. That'll still leave us wantin' for a pair of hands—
ALICE. I'll do it.
THOMAS. In a pig's eye ye will.
ALICE. Give me a reason.
THOMAS. Yer in petticoats.

ALICE. I'll break your neck.
CHARLEY. She'll do it, too.
ALICE. Harriet Blatch says—
THOMAS. Harriet Blatch? That fat sow who'll be gettin' her face in all the papers?

(CHARLEY reaches out and shakes his hand.)

CHARLEY. Thanks, mate.
THOMAS. What'll that be for?
CHARLEY. We're even.
THOMAS. All right—the lady'll be rowin'. Now what we'll be doin' is findin' ourselves a boat nobody's got to yet, then I'll be lookin' for Martin—
ALICE. Where is he?
THOMAS. Out on the deck sayin' a rosary.
MRS. STRAUS. Isn't it a little early for that?
THOMAS. He'll be all right now. Him and me, we'd be playin' foot-soldiers from the cradle, and always for him to be the one dyin' the hero. Been rehearsin' the moment for eighteen years. If indeed we'll be savin' his life, it'll likely ruin his whole day.
CHARLEY. *(To ALICE.)* Sis, me and Tom'll find Father—
THOMAS. —and the rest of ye'll wait for us in the boat.
ALICE. What if somebody tries to take your place?
THOMAS. They won't try very hard. I'll be seein' to that.
ALICE. *I'll* be seeing to that.
THOMAS. Would ye be askin' for a blackened eye?
ALICE. Would ye?

(A beat.)

THOMAS. Ye be seein' to that. *(Turning.)* Mary— *(He sees her knitting.)*. And what in Hell'd that be?
MARY. A stocking. For Mr. MacKay.
THOMAS. What'll he have, then—one foot?
MARY. I'll thank you to remember that unless me mind is otherwise changed, he's still me beloved.

THOMAS. Not in *my* lifeboat, he isn't.
ALICE. Miss Canavan?
MARY. Mary.
ALICE. You're not really going to marry a man you've never met just because he liked your photograph. Are you?
MARY. Marry him I will. And bear his children too, make no mistake.

(A pause.)

ALICE. We'll talk.

(As they all rise and prepare to leave, ASTOR turns around, puzzled.)

MRS. STRAUS. Are you all right, Colonel?
ASTOR. Haven't I forgotten something?
CHARLEY, ALICE and MRS. STRAUS. Your wife.
ASTOR. My pipe.

(Suddenly the downstage door is flung open; ISMAY shoves MURDOCH through the entrance.)

ISMAY. Tell them! Go ahead! Let them see what you've done!
MURDOCH. Mr. Ismay, it wasn't my place to question Lord Pirrie! If you recall, sir, I suggested several months ago that—
ISMAY. I SAID TELL THEM!
MRS. STRAUS. It's all right, Mr. Murdoch.
MURDOCH. Mrs. Straus, by all that's Holy, I didn't know to act differently! Because they told me she couldn't sink!
ASTOR. Bruce?
ISMAY. According to Thomas Andrews, we only have two hours left. That is, if we're fortunate.
STRAUS. But the Carpathia—
ISMAY. What about her? Even at seventeen knots, she couldn't possibly reach us before dawn.
MRS. STRAUS. Is that all? Why, Mr. Murdoch, you're not to worry for another moment. Though spending the evening in a

lifeboat is clearly something to be hidden from one's neighbors, it should prove a most original experience. Damp, perhaps, but—
ISMAY. TELL THEM!

(As MURDOCH grows more agitated, his speech begins to develop a distinct Cockney tinge.)

MURDOCH. *(To MRS. STRAUS.)* You see, Ma'am—the Board of Trade says we're required to carry twenty boats. That we do.
MRS. STRAUS. Yes?
MURDOCH. Well, at 70 passengers each, that only accounts for fourteen hundred lives saved.

(A pause.)

MRS. STRAUS. Come again?

(STRAUS turns to ASTOR.)

STRAUS. I'm beginning to hear what he's not telling us.
ASTOR. Indeed. *(To ISMAY.)* Bruce, how many people are on board this ship?
ISMAY. Twenty-two hundred. But it could have been worse!
ASTOR. HOW?!?
ISMAY. We're only two-thirds full. Another thousand might have drowned.
STRAUS. "Another thousand might have drowned." Tell me, Mr. Ismay. Do you intend to make that the company slogan?
MURDOCH. Please, Mr. Straus. The shame is mine, sir. Perhaps if I'd hit her head-on and only flooded the first compartment—
ISMAY. SHUT UP, YOU DIMWITTED BOOR!

(Mortified, MURDOCH turns his back on the others, facing upstage.)

ALICE. Well, this is just ducky.

CHARLEY. The heck it is. Ducks float.

ASTOR. Bruce, would you mind telling us what happens next? Or is that a surprise, too?

ISMAY. What do you think happens next? Rules of the sea.

CHARLEY. Does that mean—

ISMAY. It means women and children first! *(Pause.)* God help them.

STRAUS. Oh, you mean He's not on your payroll after all?

ASTOR. What about the rest of us?

ISMAY. We'll have to use our ingenuity. *Something* on this ship should be capable of remaining above water. *(Pointing.)* That chaise, for instance.

MRS. STRAUS. Mr. Ismay! As far as the Social Register is concerned, my husband and I are crossing on the Titanic. And while, under the circumstances, I'm sure they'd make allowances for the Carpathia, do you seriously expect me to tell them that we came over in a chair?!?

THOMAS. *(To MARY.)* He wouldn't be scarin' ye now, would he?

MARY. No, Thomas.

THOMAS. Hold onto me hand then. *(To ISMAY.)* Ye listen here—ye'll be watchin' what ye say around me girl.

(ISMAY turns and takes in THOMAS and MARY for the first time. There is a pause.)

ISMAY. Another pet, Colonel Astor?

ASTOR. That's enough, Ismay—

ISMAY. *(To THOMAS.)* How did you and that—that woman get up here?

THOMAS. Courtesy of me right shoulder. Ye'll not be findin' a gate from here to Hell holdin' back a Galway man with his Irish up.

ALICE. *(To MARY.)* I thought you said the gate was open!

MARY. Oh, it was. After he got through with it.

(MURDOCH turns around slowly. He's holding onto something we do not see.)

ISMAY. *(To THOMAS.)* You'll go back down below and wait your turn.
THOMAS. Let's be callin' a spade by its proper name now, mate. What turn? I been under the impression meself they had orders to shoot us on sight.
ALICE. Oh, my God.
MRS. STRAUS. That isn't true! *(To ISMAY.)* Is it?
ISMAY. Of course it isn't true. *(Pause.)* They've been told to fire a warning first. *(To THOMAS.)* Have you any idea how much these people paid for a stateroom?
THOMAS. 'Tis funny, but I'd only be payin' six and four meself. And guess what? We'll still be headin' for the same place.
ISMAY. I have no intention of explaining proper breeding to a sanctimonious immigrant who—

(MURDOCH taps him on the shoulder. He turns around to find a gun barrel pressed against his forehead.)

MURDOCH. Ponchielli wrote *La Gioconda*, you horse's ass. And if you open that latrine you call a mouth one more time, you're going to find yourself with an unexpected navel in an even more unexpected place.

(There is a deathly silence. Broken shortly by ISMAY.)

ISMAY. You're fired! *(MURDOCH cocks the hammer.)* But I'm willing to reconsider!
MURDOCH. Oh, you are? And where would you start?
ISMAY. Wherever you want. Just put the gun away.
MRS. STRAUS. Mr. Murdoch—
MURDOCH. Please, Mrs. Straus. He don't— He doesn't deserve your kindness any more than I do for obeying such as him in the first place.
ISMAY. This is *my* vessel!
MURDOCH. IS IT? IS IT? *(Pointing to the others.)* Go on—tell that to this gentleman's wife when she asks why it is she has to wear

black. Tell that to the young lady the next time she reaches for her brother only he isn't there. Of course she's going down, you ignorant piece of worm meat! What in the name of Jesus Christ did you expect? How many times do you think you can laugh at Nature before she decides it's time to laugh back? Five? Ten? A dozen? Forty-six thousand tons, indeed! Let's really show the Lord what for! *(Pause.)* There's not a liner in the fleet that wouldn't have missed that berg by half a mile with what I did to her. Not a one that wouldn't have said, "Right-o, jack tar" when I told her hard astarboard, full speed astern. But then there's the Titanic. Twice again as big as anything I've ever seen in my life. And how much time did she get to court me? How much time did I have to learn her moods, her tempers, and the way she makes love to the brine that carries her? Twenty minutes! Do you hear me? It took me a fortnight to get an automobile license, but I couldn't beg half an hour alone with my own damned ship! *(Pause.)* Only now I'm expected to go down like a noble seaman as though this was all my idea to begin with. Well, I'll tell you something, Mr. Ismay, "sir". If I *am* an imbecile as you say, that's only come about from living by your rules—and taking into account where *that's* gotten us, you'll forgive me if I choose to die by my own. But just the same, if I happen to see you in Hell, I hope you'll have the good sense to walk the other way. *(He starts to leave, then stops.)* You know—the only one who doesn't deserve this is the Titanic. *(Pause; glancing around the room.)* God might have been proud to claim her as His own if He'd just been given the chance. *(He puts his hand on the doorknob and turns, brandishing the gun.)* I trust you'll consider this my resignation from the White Star Line.

(MURDOCH exits. The others are pale. CHARLEY mumbles to himself fervently.)

CHARLEY. He's not gonna do it, he's not gonna do it, he's not gonna do it, he's—

(A gunshot from offstage. They all turn to ISMAY and glare at him coldly. For once, he has the grace to appear ashamed.)

ISMAY. *(Indicating MURDOCH.)* I—ah—apologize for the disturbance. Uh—assuming the crew haven't all jumped overboard, I'll—ah—have somebody sweep him up. *(To THOMAS.)* Get out of here. Now.

(ASTOR steps forward and speaks quietly.)

ASTOR. Bruce, if you lay one hand on him, you won't live long enough to die nobly. Do I make myself clear?

(They all turn to him, astonished.)

ISMAY. Uh—of course. *(He begins backing toward the downstage door. As he does, he sees a crooked painting on the wall, which he straightens.)* Now if—uh—you'll excuse me, I'm needed on deck. Nobody seems to know how to—uh—lower the lifeboats. Silly, isn't it? Have a pleasant evening. *(Just before he exits, he turns back and eyes them all, mumbling to himself)* Good God. I've killed George M. Cohan.

(He exits. THOMAS crosses to ASTOR and extends a hand.)

THOMAS. Mate?
ASTOR. Get away from me.

(There is dead silence as they all turn away to look at the floor, the walls, the table tops—anything to keep from facing the inevitable. In the midst of the quiet, CHARLEY clears his throat. Six heads snap up instantly and pivot to him. He shrinks back into the woodwork with an apologetic shrug.)

CHARLEY. Sorry.

(The quiet resumes for a few seconds. Then STRAUS turns to his wife.)

STRAUS. Ida, you're getting on one of those boats.

MRS. STRAUS. I assure you I'm doing nothing of the kind.
STRAUS. Dammit, woman—I don't have time to argue.
MRS. STRAUS. Then we're in complete agreement.

(ALICE turns to CHARLEY and reaches for him.)

ALICE. Charley—
CHARLEY. He said women and children only!
ALICE. Women and children *first*! We'll get around it. You act like you're twelve anyway. If they want proof, just open your mouth and say something. They'll never know the difference.
MARY. Thomas, put on your coat. Quickly!
THOMAS. Might we be talkin' about this?
MARY. There isn't time! Hurry!
THOMAS. Mary, can I be makin' a confession? I never been in a rowboat in me life. I get seasick.
STRAUS. Ida, for God's sake, listen to reason—
ALICE. Charley, just stay behind me. I'll do the talking—
THOMAS. Mary—
CHARLEY. Alice—
MRS. STRAUS. Isidor—

(Suddenly, ASTOR breaks into peals of laughter. The others stop cold and turn to him. There is a frightened beat.)

STRAUS. Just as I feared. Panic has driven him insane.
MRS. STRAUS. Should I get him some water?
STRAUS. I think that's been taken care of, don't you?
ASTOR. *(Gasping.)* God, it's just too asinine! Thousands of dollars to cross the sea, and nothing works! What do you suppose they'll discover next? That the lifeboats leak?

(He's off again. ALICE addresses him coldly.)

ALICE. I'm sure there's nothing amusing about—
ASTOR. Of course it's amusing. How could it be anything but? The floating palace! Mankind's greatest achievement! Yet all the

king's horses and all the king's men knew better. They've gone to lunch. Tell me, Straus. Are you familiar with the word "ubris"?

STRAUS. I—

ASTOR. Certainly you are. The Greeks were quite fond of it as well. Particularly when they'd put their foot in it one time too many. It was the price they paid for their own insolence—and evidently it didn't die with Sophocles after all. You can take off the coat, Mrs. Straus. Because it's much too late.

(THOMAS instantly turns to MARY and begins pushing her out the door.)

THOMAS. Gerup.
MARY. Thomas, what'll you be doin'?
THOMAS. There'll be a hatmaker waitin' in San Francisco. Ye'll fall in love, ye'll marry him, and with luck ye'll be havin' lots of *little* hats—
MARY. Aren't you comin' with me?
THOMAS. He wouldn't be fancyin' that at all. I chew in me sleep....

(They're out the door, which slams shut behind them. There's a pause.)

ASTOR. And that's the last we'll see of Mr. Kilgannon.
STRAUS. I question your faith in human nature.
ASTOR. And I pity yours.
MRS. STRAUS. Come now. At least the young man had the decency to see her to safety. That's more than can be said for the well-being of your bride.
ASTOR. Nonsense. He's just as myopic as we are. Where in Hell is it written that the only wisdom on this planet lies with the poor but honest? And dammit—why are they invariably Irish?
ALICE. Charley—
CHARLEY. *(To ALICE.)* Sis, what did he mean—"We only have two hours left"?
ASTOR. He meant we're sinking, Charles! Is that plain enough

for you? And nobody's exempt this time—not even a real live nephew of his Uncle Sam. Because by tomorrow morning, the last generation of the deaf, dumb and blind will be lying two miles deep on the ocean floor!

(A deathly pause.)

STRAUS. Well, that's *one* way to get rid of the band.
ASTOR. Oh, for God's sake, Straus. You needn't act so damned complacent.
STRAUS. And you needn't act so incredulous. You haven't deceived anyone, you know.
ASTOR. Pardon me, but I *am* incredulous. This is hardly an eventuality I was bred to anticipate.
STRAUS. Then why did you put Mrs. Astor on a lifeboat an hour ago? Are you that bored? *(Mumbling.)* Eavesdropping on the wireless, indeed....
ASTOR. Do you really think I'd subject her to this? Do you? And what about my unborn son? *He* didn't orchestrate this idiotic apocalypse, did he? *(Pause.)* If I had even a shred of nobility, I'd have plunged in after them. Unfortunately, any morals I may have once owned were purchased years ago along with my bank notes—so I suppose the hero's gesture will have to suffice. Even if some of us know better. *(Whirling.)* AND I'D HAVE GIVEN HER MY JUMPER, TOO—IF I HAD ONE!
MRS. STRAUS. I— I didn't know. I'm sorry.
ASTOR. Yes, everybody's sorry, aren't they? You are, I am—so is that poor devil with the bullet in his head. He was quite right, you know. The only one who doesn't deserve this is the ship.
STRAUS. And for your part, what would you have done differently?
ASTOR. Nothing. But I always assumed I'd have the intelligence to see it coming in time. *(Pause.)* Which, I suppose, is just as arrogant as all the rest. *(Pause.)* God, I wish it weren't too late to make a difference!

(ALICE crosses downstage to ASTOR and puts a hand on his arm.)

ALICE. Corporal—
ASTOR. "Captain."
CHARLEY. *(Mumbling.)* "Colonel."
ALICE. *(Gently.)* She might have a daughter.
ASTOR. I beg your pardon?
ALICE. Your wife.
ASTOR. She wouldn't dare. I credit her with a great deal more sense than that.
ALICE. It would hardly be considered an affliction, you know.
ASTOR. Indeed it would! A boy can take care of himself. But a little girl? Utterly helpless, I assure you. I'll never understand the willingness of some men to put up with the endless tears a son would have the decency to keep to himself. My God, have you seen what goes on? You're forced to pass judgment on everything from a skinned knee to a bee sting, to the point where the child becomes the cynosure of your entire existence. Nothing else seems to matter. Yet, who's to take care of her—who's to take your place—if something should happen to *you*? *(Pause.)* A man would have to be a perfect fool.
ALICE. How old is she?
ASTOR. Who?
ALICE. Your little girl.

(ASTOR turns away. There is a pause.)

ASTOR. Ten.
ALICE. What's her name?

(A beat.)

ASTOR. It's Alice.

(There is a sudden explosion from outside as one last flare goes off. They all turn toward the portholes; MRS. STRAUS moves to the nearest one and peers out.)

STRAUS. *(Indicating the flare.)* Again with the rocket. What do

they expect from us—a National Anthem?
MRS. STRAUS. *(At the window.)* Goodbye. *(Waving.)* See you soon. *(Another wave.)* Toodle-oo. Have a safe trip.
STRAUS. What in the name of God are you doing?
MRS. STRAUS. Alice, dear—come quickly and see what Renée Harris calls an evening coat. Were I her, I'd prefer sinking to being caught in public wearing that.
STRAUS. IDA, GET ON THAT BOAT!
MRS. STRAUS. Isidor, sit! *(Pointing.)* She's holding onto that paddle, in the third one from the left. Right between Mrs. Widener and Mr. Ismay.
ALL. WHAT?

(The others race to the portholes.)

CHARLEY. I thought he was gonna use his ingenuity!
ALICE. Apparently, he doesn't have any.
CHARLEY. Wasn't he just supposed to help lower them?
ALICE. Yeah. From the inside.
ASTOR. That blackguard!
STRAUS. That scoundrel.
MRS. STRAUS. That son-of-a-bitch.
THOMAS. *(Re-entering.)* And I'd barely be comin' through the door yet.

(They all turn to stare. THOMAS is standing in the doorway in pants and shoes only—barechested from having wrapped MARY in his jacket and shirt.)

STRAUS. Surprising to have you back, Mr. Kilgannon. *(Deliberately.) Isn't* it, Colonel Astor?
THOMAS. Sure ye'd be keepin' the cork in the bottle then, for it wouldn't be over yet. *(To ALICE.)* Gerup, yer next. Yer Mum and sisters'd be floatin' out there already.
ALICE. What about Father?
CHARLEY. How do you know it was them?
THOMAS. Half'd be callin' for "Alice," and the other half'd be

shoutin' "Charley". True I wouldn't be havin' much of an education now, but that still won't be stoppin' one and one from turnin' up two. *(To ASTOR; snapping his fingers.)* Coat for the lady, mate. It'll be thinkin' it's January out there bye and bye.

ALICE. Don't be silly. I'll wear my brother's. *(Reaching for him.)* Come on, Charley.

(THOMAS grabs hold of ALICE's hand.)

THOMAS. I wouldn't be sayin' *him* now, would I?

ALICE. Let go! *(To CHARLEY.)* Charley, would you please tell him that— *(She pulls free of THOMAS and sees the expression on her brother's face.)* Oh, no.

CHARLEY. Sis, I have to stay.

ALICE. Don't be silly, Charley. You're a baby. They can't do this to you.

CHARLEY. They already have. Now, look—I'll be on the next boat. I promise. Why don't you just find Mother and Ethel and—

ALICE. No. Wait. Let me think. Uh—you go and I'll stay here. If anybody asks, I'll tell them I'm taking your place.

CHARLEY. It doesn't work that way.

ALICE. It doesn't? *(Pointing to MRS. STRAUS.)* She's not leaving.

CHARLEY. That's different.

ALICE. Why? Just because she's an old woman?

MRS. STRAUS. *(Mumbling.)* If she calls me that one more time....

THOMAS. Come on, Alice. Ye'd only be makin' it harder.

ALICE. LET GO OF ME!

THOMAS. I said—

ALICE. DON'T YOU UNDERSTAND?! HE'S MY BROTHER!

THOMAS. Ye'll not be the only one sayin' goodbye, ye know! And be thankin' the Almighty for that! Some'll be washed over before they even have the chance!

ALICE. I'M NOT GOING TO LET THAT HAPPEN TO CHARLEY!

CHARLEY. YOU THINK YOU CAN CHANGE THAT, TOO,

ALICE?

ALICE. I CAN TRY, CAN'T I? *(Beginning to cry.)* If I leave, who's going to take care of you....

(He puts his arms around her and hugs her tightly.)

CHARLEY. Boy, and you call *me* dumb.
ALICE. I never called you dumb.
CHARLEY. You always call me dumb.
ALICE. "Thick". I called you thick. There's a difference.
CHARLEY. Well, you picked a heck of a time to tell me that.
ALICE. And you picked a heck of a time to grow up. Of all the bone-headed, half-witted stunts you've ever pulled—
CHARLEY. Yeah. This is worse than when I gave the piano player your music upside down.
ALICE. This is worse than when you told that rugby captain I had leprosy.
CHARLEY. I bet it's even worse than the time I tried to sell you to Mrs. Coates for a quarter.
ALICE. No. It's not worse than that. *That* was the worst thing you ever did to me.
CHARLEY. How come? She took the refund!

(ALICE pulls away.)

ALICE. Are you going to let me stay?
CHARLEY. No!
ALICE. Why?!
CHARLEY. You have to pitch!
ALICE. We have an audition! I *don't* have to pitch!
CHARLEY. Like hell you don't!
ALICE. I thought you were jealous!
CHARLEY. Who said I was jealous?!
ALICE. Who had to?!
CHARLEY. So what! You think you'll get the vote like this? By croaking in the middle of nowhere? You think that'll make a difference to anyone? Alice, for Pete's sake, nobody's gonna

remember what happened here tonight. It won't mean a thing! Unless you *do* stay. And then all's it'll mean is that Harriet Blatch has to start over again. Don't you see? It isn't worth it!

(ALICE begins to crack.)

    ALICE. Oh, Charley—*you* are.

(They're in each other's arms. He's holding onto her for dear life.)

    CHARLEY. Sis, I love you so much. *(Pause.)* And if I *was* jealous, it was for all the right reasons. Honest. Will you promise me you won't forget that?

(ALICE pulls away. She is sobbing.)

    ALICE. Charley—remember all those times when I said—when I said you couldn't live without me?
    CHARLEY. So?
    ALICE. You don't have to prove it. I'm—I'm willing to admit I was wrong.
    CHARLEY. Look, what I want you to do is go to the audition and tell Mr. Cohan I may be a little late. Okay? And if I'm not there in time, start with "Harrigan". You don't need me for that one. *(ALICE nods. She kisses him on the cheek, then turns around and starts for the door.)* Alice—

(She's back in his arms for one last embrace.)

    ALICE. Take care of Father.
    CHARLEY. I will.

(Then she breaks it with finality and opens the downstage door. THOMAS holds out his hand as if to lead her to the boat deck; ALICE pushes it away.)

    ALICE. *I* can find it.

(And she's gone. After a long moment, CHARLEY crosses upstage to the piano and sits on the bench, his back to the others, and buries his face in his hands. STRAUS turns to his wife and indicates CHARLEY.)

STRAUS. Ida—

(MRS. STRAUS rises and crosses upstage to CHARLEY. She puts her arms around him from behind and attempts to console him. ASTOR nods toward CHARLEY.)

ASTOR. If my son Vincent becomes half the man he is, I hope someone sees fit to give me the credit.
STRAUS. Indeed. Though I must confess, I never thought he had it in him.
THOMAS. Me neither, old salt. He'd always be strikin' me a bit on the dandy side. What with how he'll be dressin' and all.

(There is a pause. STRAUS sits at the down left table; THOMAS and ASTOR stare at each other from opposite sides of the stage. After a moment, ASTOR crosses slowly to THOMAS until they are face-to-face. This is clearly the hardest thing he's ever had to do in his life. Following a beat, he points to the boat deck.)

ASTOR. You saw me out there earlier, didn't you?
THOMAS. Yes.
ASTOR. I'm curious. Why have you kept your mouth shut?
THOMAS. Ye'd be doin' enough talkin' for the both of us, wouldn't ye? And the night'll be short enough as 'tis.
ASTOR. I didn't get into the boat with her! I only asked! She is, after all, pregnant.
THOMAS. Ye don't be owin' me an explanation now. I'll be just as frightened as you—and if she'd be me own Missus, I'd have been attemptin' the same.
ASTOR. Oh, come off it, Kilgannon. Even if I *didn't* lie professionally I'd see through that one.

THOMAS. Sure it's what ye'll be wantin' to hear though, isn't it?

(A pause.)

ASTOR. I'm afraid I owe you a rather substantial apology. If you'll accept it.
THOMAS. No, ye don't, mate. 'Tis me own fault for sayin' me piece with me heart instead of me brains. Got it from me Mum. The Killaleas'd be speakin' their minds from 1642 and they wouldn't be satisfied yet.
ASTOR. Well, naturally, when I—when you appeared in that ridiculous-looking attire—not even a waistcoat, for God's sake—of course I assumed that—
THOMAS. —it'll be me before the others? I wouldn't be standin' for that now. Me nephew Michael'd be lookin' up to me, don't ye know—and I'll be havin' him to think about, too. *(Pause.)* I only wanted to get meself upstairs that I might be havin' a fighter's chance like any other man. And if that means I'll be puttin' on studs and a wing-tip to get me just due as one who'll be better than most and no worse than some—well, mate. We'll all be dressin' up in one thing or another now, won't we? *(Pointing to ASTOR's clothing.)* Only suits like that, they don't be comin' cheap. Not in Corrafarry anyways.
ASTOR. And you really think that's all it takes?
THOMAS. Let's be puttin' it this way, then. I wouldn't be seein' nothin' yet to change me mind—and I'll be givin' it twenty-two years the sixth of May next.

(ASTOR smiles slightly, then crosses to the center stage table, where he pulls out a checkbook and begins to write.)

ASTOR. "Kilgannon" has two n's, doesn't it?
THOMAS. And another who'll be comin' after the o. Why? What'll ye be doin'?

(ASTOR removes the check and hands it to him.)

ASTOR. Congratulations, Thomas. You're a millionaire. Now tell me—do you think it'll help you get off this boat?

STRAUS. Colonel Astor, have you gone mad? Suppose he cashes it?

ASTOR. Suppose he does? The implications make the risk worthwhile.

(THOMAS looks up from the check, astounded.)

THOMAS. Is this good?

ASTOR. *(To STRAUS.)* See? He's a natural. *(To THOMAS.)* What do *you* think?

THOMAS. I think ye'd be tryin' to hang me by me own principles.

ASTOR. Precisely. And it always works, so don't fight it. Haven't you ever been tempted before?

THOMAS. Only by Satan!

ASTOR. That's all right. My influence is much greater, and I'm a lot wealthier.

STRAUS. He is, too.

THOMAS. And this is what ye'd be doin' for a livin' then?

STRAUS. No, he counts his father's money for a living.

ASTOR. *(To STRAUS.)* Which is no more ignoble than selling coffee tables. *(There is a challenging pause as ASTOR turns to THOMAS.)* What sayest thou, Tom? Do I win?

(THOMAS stares down at the check, then back at ASTOR.)

THOMAS. No.

ASTOR. *(Looking heavenward.)* Thank God! There's hope for the world yet!

THOMAS. Ye'll be wantin' me to give it back, then?

ASTOR. I wouldn't hear of it. And if it'll make your nephew Michael think all the more of you, you can call it my tuition.

THOMAS. I don't be followin' ye now. That'd be payment for an education.

ASTOR. I'm aware of that. You want a drink?

THOMAS. Would ye be buyin'?
ASTOR. You learn quickly, don't you?
THOMAS. Indeed. I'd be getting' that from the Killaleas, too. What'll ye be havin'?
ASTOR. Whisky and soda.
THOMAS. Two, then.
ASTOR. Straus?

(There is a dumbfounded pause.)

STRAUS. Well, this is the most unlikely sight I've witnessed yet. What's next, Colonel? Barn dancing?

(ASTOR crosses up to the bar as THOMAS moves to the down left table and sits with STRAUS.)

ASTOR. Remarkable, isn't it? If such things can be done in the dead of night in mid-Atlantic, what *can't* be done under more favorable circumstances?
STRAUS. Meaning what?
ASTOR. Meaning I wish I held stock in Marconi wireless. After this evening, it's going to skyrocket.
THOMAS. Please, mate—don't be talkin' skyrockets. If I had to be takin' off me shirt one more time, me arms'd be locked at the elbows. Where'd they be findin' this weather anyways?
STRAUS. Why don't you ask the Colonel? One of his relatives probably owns it.

(THOMAS looks around to make sure no one can hear him, then leans in and whispers to STRAUS.)

THOMAS. Mr. Straus?
STRAUS. What happened to "old salt"?
THOMAS. I think I'd be tradin' it in for me workin' papers. *(Pause.)* What's Yom Kippur now?
STRAUS. Confession, wholesale.

(ASTOR returns to the table with two glasses. He is joined by MRS. STRAUS.)

ASTOR. *(Indicating CHARLEY.)* How is he?
MRS. STRAUS. How do you think? That poor child. There was nothing I could possibly say.
STRAUS. That's never stopped you before.
THOMAS. I wouldn't be takin' it much to heart, Bridey. This'd be no night for happy endings now, would it?
ASTOR. *(Looking up.)* No?

(They all turn around. MARY is standing in the doorway, wearing THOMAS' coat and shirt over her dress. THOMAS rises, transfixed, as she points upstage to where she had been sitting.)

MARY. I—I forgot me stocking. *(She crosses up center to retrieve it, turns, and begins to exit. She has passed THOMAS by two paces before she stops and faces him.)* But p'raps as long as I'm here—

(And he has her in his arms, his mouth covering hers. After a moment, he pulls back.)

THOMAS. And what about the hatmaker?
MARY. What about him? Me Mum taught me nothin' of hats. Supposin' he should strike up a conversation about derbies? Now what would I say to him, tell me that?
THOMAS. Mary, ye wouldn't be wantin' to marry *me* now, would ye?
MARY. Oh, Thomas—if you can find a way to make that possible, I'll do it twice. And that's the truth.
THOMAS. I'll be goin' to work on it.
MARY. Well, then, it would be me great honor, Mr. Kilgannon.

(Another kiss. But a deep one.)

MRS. STRAUS. We really ought to find some rice, don't you

think? Perhaps if the kitchen is still open—
 STRAUS. What good would *that* do? Unless you intend to throw oysters....
 THOMAS. *(To MARY.)* And why wouldn't ye be sayin' yes before? I'd nearly be breakin' me back tryin'.
 MARY. You never asked me!
 THOMAS. Indeed I did! *(Pause.)* Didn't I?

(She leads him to the table.)

MARY. Oh, you may have said somethin' about sleepin' on the floor, as though we were livin' in sin—but this is America, Thomas. Harriet Stanton Blatch says—
 ASTOR and STRAUS. Oh, no....
 MRS. STRAUS. My dear, I have a sapphire that would look absolutely lovely with your coloring. You must let me give it to you as a wedding gift.
 STRAUS. You won't have the time. You're getting on one of those boats. *(MRS. STRAUS glares at him. He looks heavenward.)* I did my best. You created her.
 MARY. Thomas, you don't suppose your brother would mind, do you?
 THOMAS. Forget me brother, for I'll be buyin' you a whole house.
 MARY. And with what, do you think?
 THOMAS. Mary, I—
 MARY. You'll be sellin' stocks for Mr. Straus, or whatever it is a stock boy does—
 STRAUS. *(To ASTOR.)* Perhaps I'll start him in the mailroom instead. There's a lower threshold of disappointment.
 ASTOR. Indeed.
 MARY. *(To THOMAS.)* —and I'll take in sewin' at the church where I'll be teachin'—
 THOMAS. Ye won't be havin' to—
 MARY. But I want to, Thomas. It isn't a marriage if you won't let me do for you as well. Oh, it'll be grand.
 THOMAS. But I—I mean— *(He stares at her for a long*

moment, then turns to ASTOR and hands him the check.) Sorry, mate. I believe I'll be costin' more than this after all.
 ASTOR. How *much* more?
 THOMAS. Ye couldn't be affordin' me now.

(ASTOR picks up the cards.)

 ASTOR. Then might I interest you in winning it?
 THOMAS. Ye'd be treadin' dangerous close to me principles again. *(Pause.)* But I'll deal.

(As THOMAS deals them each a hand, CHARLEY turns around slowly on the piano bench upstage. After a moment, he begins to accompany himself absently.)

 CHARLEY. "Did you ever see two Yankees part upon a foreign shore? When the good ship's just about to start for old New York once more. With tear-dimmed eye they say goodbye, They're friends without a doubt. Then the man on the pier shouts, "let "er all clear"—as the ship.... strikes.... out...."

(He carelessly starts playing the melody to "Give My Regards to Broadway" as the lights suddenly flicker. Those at the table look up instantly. There is a pause.)

 MRS. STRAUS. How entirely thoughtless. They really might have warned us, you know.
 STRAUS. What did you expect them to do—advertise it in the New York Times? "Sails April tenth, sinks on the fifteenth"?
 MRS. STRAUS. Why not? If I'd known I was going to perish, I'd have worn my good jewelry.
 THOMAS. *(To ASTOR.)* Ye don't suppose we ought to be makin' a run for it, do ye mate?
 STRAUS. Certainly not. It isn't dignified. One of these days, you must allow us to teach you propriety.
 THOMAS. I'll have to be learnin' to spell it first.
 STRAUS. We'll take care of that, too.

ASTOR. Besides, if we sit here patiently and wait, I'm sure help will be along presently.
MARY. And what if it isn't, would you mind sayin'?
ASTOR. What then? Aren't you prepared?

(She reaches for THOMAS' hand.)

MARY. Except for leavin' me baggage downstairs....

(STRAUS turns to his wife.)

STRAUS. What about you, my dear? You'd best speak up. *(Pause.)* Have you any regrets?
MRS. STRAUS. One. *(Pause.)* I so wanted to be present the day they made Alfred Hess walk the plank.
STRAUS. ALFRED HESS IS A FINE MAN!
MRS. STRAUS. Yes, I'm sure he is. For a bandit. *(Pause.)* And—well, I did hope we'd have another ten years.
STRAUS. For God's sake, why? Can you imagine me in another ten years?
MRS. STRAUS. Can you imagine *me*?

(He takes her hand.)

STRAUS. I really wouldn't worry, my dear. After all—who needs five honeymoons?
MRS. STRAUS. Oh, Isidor. I'd have settled for two.

(ASTOR throws in a card.)

ASTOR. I'll raise you.
THOMAS. I'll be through, then.
MARY. Another, please.
STRAUS. Ida?
MRS. STRAUS. How should *I* know? All he gave me were queens.

(The others groan and throw in their cards. As ASTOR reshuffles, CHARLEY begins singing energetically to himself, with a vigor that almost borders on rage.)

CHARLEY. "Whisper of how I'm yearning, To mingle with the old-time throng. Yes, give my regards to old Broadway—"

(ASTOR turns upstage, holding the cards.)

ASTOR. Are you in, Charley?

(A beat.)

CHARLEY. Yeah. *(He looks back down at the piano, banging out the crescendo forcefully.)* "And say that I'll— be— there— 'ere— long...."

(As he plays the final chord, and the others lean in over their cards...)

THE CURTAIN FALLS

POSTSCRIPT

The end came at 2:20 a.m.

Alice Fortune and J. Bruce Ismay sought refuge in two of the Titanic's twenty lifeboats. They, along with 701 others, were rescued at daybreak by the Cunard liner Carpathia, whose captain, Arthur Rostron, had raced her through the night across the 58 seemingly endless miles.

First Officer William Murdoch committed suicide on the gently sloping decks of the ship he had, for a brief time, called home.

Charley Fortune, John Jacob Astor, Isidor Straus, Ida Straus, Thomas Kilgannon, and Mary Canavan all chose to remain with the Titanic for her last noble ride.

PROPERTY PLOT

Four candelabras affixed to the walls
Framed paintings of seaports and sailing vessels
Chandelier
Silver tray with liquor bottles
Liquor glasses
Silver ice bucket and tongs
Pocket watch (Astor)
Pipee and Tobacco (Astor)
Deck of playing cards
Coins
Inkwell and pen on card table
Crystal lamps on end tables
Candelabra on piano
Telegram (Charley)
Lifejacket
Piece of paper with Morse code (Astor)
Piece of paper with address (Mary)
Knitting needles and sock (Mary)
Handkerchief (Mary)
Pistol (Murdoch)
Checkbook (Astor)

COSTUME PLOT

JOHN JACOB ASTOR and ISIDOR STRAUS: Formal dinner attire with suspenders, cummerbund and dark shoes

J. BRUCE ISMAY: Tuxedo

FIRST OFFICER WILLIAM MURDOCH: Navy blue officer's uniform with gold buttons and braid; officer's cap

ALICE FORTUNE: Floor-length light blue evening gown, pearl choker, white gloves

CHARLEY FORTUNE: White pants, white shirt, red-and-white striped vest, blue bow tie with white polka dots, straw boater, and song-and-dance man's cane

THOMAS KILGANNON: Worker's pants, jumper and boots; ill-fitting tuxedo with suspenders

IDA STRAUS: Black evening dress with trim; pearl necklace

MARY CANAVAN: Floor-length homemade dress frayed along the hem; shawl with hood

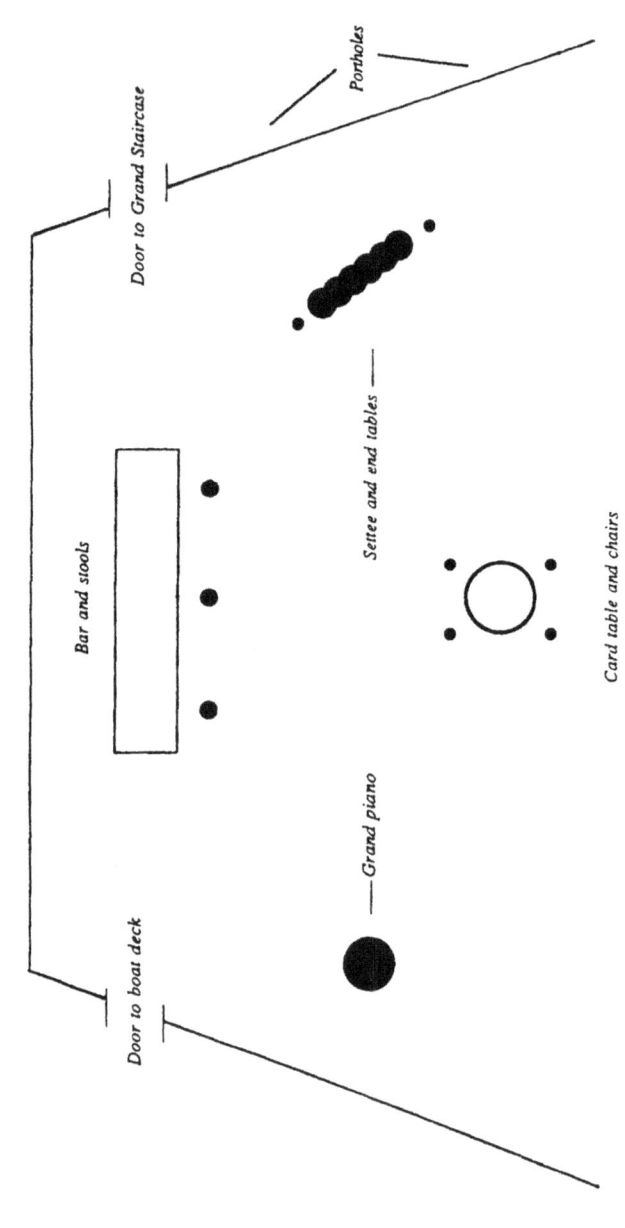

www.ingramcontent.com/pod-product-compliance
Lightning Source LLC
Chambersburg PA
CBHW072016290426
44109CB00018B/2254